THE COMPLETE IDIOT'S GUIDE® TO

Labrador Retrievers

by Margaret H. Bonham

ALPHA
A member of Penguin Group (USA) Inc.

To Larry, as always. And to the brave search-and-rescue people and dogs, the heroes of 9-11.

International Standard Book Number: 0-02-864406-9
Library of Congress Catalog Card Number: 2002110190

05 04 03 8 7 6 5 4 3 2

Interpretation of the printing code: The rightmost number of the first series of numbers is the year of the book's printing; the rightmost number of the second series of numbers is the number of the book's printing. For example, a printing code of 02-1 shows that the first printing occurred in 2002.

Printed in the United States of America

Publisher: *Marie Butler-Knight*
Product Manager: *Phil Kitchel*
Managing Editor: *Jennifer Chisholm*
Acquisitions Editor: *Mike Sanders*
Development Editor: *Lori Cates Hand*
Production Editor: *Katherin Bidwell*
Copy Editor: *Michael Dietsch*
Illustrator: *Chris Eliopoulos*
Cover/Book Designer: *Trina Wurst*
Indexer: *Angie Bess*
Layout/Proofreading: *Angela Calvert, Megan Douglass*

Contents at a Glance

Contents

Appendixes

Foreword

You're taking the plunge. Are you ready? Getting a dog is fun, exciting, and terrifying. What will my new dog be like? Will the dog love me? Will I be a good parent? Will my new dog destroy my house?

There is, of course, no guarantee to any of these questions, but one of the best indicators of your dog's personality will be his parents (not unlike humans, although this is something that few of us care to admit)!

When getting ready to adopt your Labrador Retriever puppy, go to a reputable breeder. Do *not* go to a pet store! Why? Reputable breeders care about their dogs and can give you information about the new member of your family that a pet store cannot, particularly when it comes to lineage and temperament. With a good breeder, you will be able to meet Mom and Dad Labrador. Good breeders will interview *you.* That's right, interview you! They will want to know all about your life. They will want to know how much time you will devote to the love, care, and exercise of your Lab. A store just wants to make the sale. And when you meet your puppy's parents, you will get an indication whether this is the dog you want to be with for the next 15 years. The information and education a good breeder can provide to you about your Lab will help you make an informed decision—a decision that should last a lifetime. Dogs are for life, not just for now.

Labs are a versatile, warm, funny, and loving breed, set apart from other breeds by their intelligence, good looks, and athleticism. Labs can do it all—they can guide a person, snag a Frisbee, catch a ball, search for and find missing people, swim like a fish, star in obedience, assist the disabled, sniff out danger, shine in a conformation ring, mark and retrieve a bird, and cuddle when needed (and then be happy to eat the leftovers.) I wish I were a Labrador!

And while they are *great* dogs, they are not great dogs for everyone. It is important to do your homework in selecting the right breed.

And this is why *The Complete Idiot's Guide to Labrador Retrievers* is a must read for anyone considering bringing a Lab into their home.

Is your life ready for a new dog, and a Lab at that? Time and resources are a must for this all-important new member of the family. Do you have the time to housetrain your puppy? Are you ready to brush his teeth and trim his nails? Do you have any idea how to "puppy proof" your home? Don't even think that a short stroll around the yard or up the block will be adequate exercise for this natural athlete. And what about when you go to work? How long is your Lab going to be alone? Is it too long? What is considered too long?

Are you ready to go through the fun and sometimes trying adventure of obedience training? Labradors are smart and quick. Are you? Are you willing to give your puppy the best and put his needs first? If you are unsure whether you are ready to take on this responsibility, you should wait. Do not rush into a decision about getting a dog, especially a high-energy breed like a Lab. They deserve the best, because they give the best. There *is* a reason why they are the most popular breed!

If after much thought and a long discussion with all the other members of the household (especially the cat), the decision is still a resounding "Yes," settle in for an excellent, informative, and educational read by Margaret H. Bonham.

The Complete Idiot's Guide to Labrador Retrievers will help ease the terrifying trials of raising a puppy and guide the fun for you and your new Lab. It offers full explanations on everything from housetraining and puppyhood through adolescence and adulthood. *The Complete Idiot's Guide to Labrador Retrievers* is that all-knowing, informative voice you need—from finding the right dog, to feeding, training, and understanding your Lab— and offers a realistic view of all the possible ups and downs of a canine/human relationship. This book will become your manual of what to do as the proud parent of the most popular dog on the block. When in doubt, bring this book out!

For the last 16 years as a professional dog trainer and behavioral consultant, I have had the pleasure of working and playing with dozens and dozens of Labs. Two labs at play are a sight to behold. It's as if they have an understanding of their uniqueness and charm. They *are* the celebrities of the dog world!

Little in life brings more joy than a healthy, happy, well-mannered dog, and with *The Complete Idiot's Guide to Labrador Retrievers*, you will have the power and knowledge to do the right thing for you and your dog. You both deserve it. Congratulations and let the fun begin!

Stacy Alldredge
Owner
Who's Walking Who Dog Obedience & Behavioral Training
212-414-1551
wwwdogs@aol.com

Introduction

So you want to own a Labrador Retriever? Labs are the most popular dog in the United States today and make great pets—but they're not for everyone. In this book, you'll learn a bit more about the Labrador Retriever and find out whether there's a Lab in your future.

In this book, you'll learn all about the basics of Lab ownership and what you need to do to find and raise a well-adjusted and healthy Labrador Retriever. Unlike many books that focus on top breeders and lists of dog show champions, this book focuses on the everyday aspects of Lab ownership. After all, what use are lists of dogs you've never heard of when you're trying to housebreak your puppy?

What You'll Find in This Book

This book is intended for both the first-time Lab owner and the Lab owner who is looking for tips on caring for and training their Labrador Retriever.

This book is divided into four user-friendly parts. I start by giving you an overview of the Labrador Retriever, his personality, and whether a Lab is right for you. I then continue with how to select the right Lab for you. Don't skip this part; your choices will affect your Lab's health and personality for years to come. Training is vitally important with a big dog such as the Labrador Retriever, and the book covers this thoroughly. I then move on to health and nutrition topics, including caring for your older dog.

Here's the book in a nutshell:

Part 1, "Lab Experiments," provides a basic overview of the Labrador Retriever as a breed. It discusses the commitment Lab ownership requires and helps you decide whether the Lab is the right breed for you.

Part 2, "Lab Assignments," discusses what a reputable breeder is and how to find the perfect Lab for you. It explains vital health certifications and papers that your puppy should have. It also covers selecting your Lab and dog supplies. I also discuss bringing your Lab home and the first few days with your new companion.

Part 3, "Dog Training 101," provides a basic overview of obedience training and other forms of dog training. In this section, you'll learn about pack behavior and how your Lab actually thinks. You'll find out whether it's better to find a professional trainer or "go it alone." You'll also learn about dog sports such as retrieving, agility, and tracking.

Part 4, "In Sickness and in Health," provides an overview of how to maintain your Lab's health. You'll be surprised to learn that all dog food is not created equal and that your care will help improve your Lab's life. You'll also learn about genetic diseases and what constitutes an emergency. Lastly, you'll learn how to make your Lab's senior years healthy and happy.

Extras

Check out the sidebars throughout the book. They're packed full of fun and informative facts:

Retriever Rewards

Great tips that will make your life easier.

Lab Lingo

Definitions of terms used in this book.

Lab Bites

Warnings about possible problems that might arise. Read these boxes carefully!

Lab Facts

Interesting facts about dogs in general or Labrador Retrievers in particular.

Acknowledgments

Books don't appear out of thin air. This one certainly hasn't. I'm grateful to the help and guidance of the following people (in no particular order):

- Larry Bonham, my full-time husband and part-time editor. Couldn't do it without you.
- Deb Eldredge D.V.M., both technical editor and friend. This woman read my book standing up, after being thrown from a horse and cracking her ribs. Talk about dedication! Thanks for the job lead. I appreciate it. Also to Beth Adelman, my other technical editor and friend. Thank you for editing this book, plus thanks for the contacts to the AKC.
- Jessica Faust of Bookends, Inc. Thanks for the job!
- Christine Vrba, artist and fellow dog writer.
- Ron Rella and Neil Singer of the American Kennel Club for the AKC documentation reprinted in this book.
- Andrea Reust and Peter Rapalus of Canine Companions for Independence for their photographs of working Labs. CCI is a nonprofit organization. To learn more about them, visit them at www.caninecompanions.org or contact them at Canine Companions for Independence, PO Box 446, Santa Rosa, CA 95402-0446.
- The good people on LABRADOR-L mailing list who were gracious enough to answer my questions—especially to listowners Cindy Tittle Moore and Lisa Lee Miller, who allowed me on board.
- Kent and Donna Dannen, photographers, for their stunning photos. Deepest thanks to the others who submitted photos, including Jacky Sachs, Debra Su Stephens, and Katherine Shaver for their photos that they've let me reprint in this book.

- Mike Sanders, acquisitions editor for *The Complete Idiot's Guide* series, Lori Cates Hand, development editor, and Kathy Bidwell, production editor, for their terrific work.
- The Labrador Retriever Club, for allowing the reprint of their standard.
- The good folks at Orthopedic Foundation for Animals (OFA) and Canine Eye Registration Foundation (CERF) for allowing me to reprint their certifications in this book.
- Kim Thornton, fellow dog writer and brainstormer. She and I worked on different *Complete Idiot's Guides* at the same time. Buy her book, *The Complete Idiot's Guide to Beagles*.

Special Thanks to the Technical Reviewers

The Complete Idiot's Guide to Labrador Retrievers was reviewed by experts who double-checked the accuracy of what you'll learn here, to help us ensure that this book gives you everything you need to know about Labs. Special thanks are extended to Debra Eldredge, D.V.M., and Beth Adelman.

Trademarks

Part 1

Lab Experiments

Owning a Labrador Retriever can be a great joy in your life. Labs make great companions and tireless workers. Their versatility makes them a wonderful choice for a family pet, a hunting companion, an assistance dog, a search-and-rescue dog, or a therapy dog.

Indeed, Labs are the most popular dog breed, with over 150,000 registrations yearly with the American Kennel Club. But Labs aren't for everyone.

Part 1 talks about the Labrador Retriever's personality, characteristics, and history. You'll find out whether you're ready to take the plunge into Lab ownership. Then you'll see how to pick the right dog from the right source.

Chapter 1

Labs 101

In This Chapter

- Why Labs are so dog-gone popular
- Lab personality basics
- Bringing a Lab into your life
- Why Labs are the do-it-all dog
- Some heroic and celebrity Labs
- A short history of the Lab

The Labrador Retriever is the most popular purebred dog in the United States. The versatility and friendliness of this breed make the Lab an ideal companion as both a pet and a willing worker. In this chapter, you'll find out whether a Lab is right for you. Although the Labrador Retriever is an easygoing breed and relatively easy to train, the Lab is not for everyone. We'll explore the Lab personality and the time commitment necessary for owning a Labrador Retriever.

We'll also look at the versatility of the Labrador Retriever. Labs are routinely used in search-and-rescue, therapy, assistance, and police work. Labs are still great hunting companions and have proven themselves in the field.

The history of the Labrador is what has shaped this wonderful breed. You may be surprised to learn that the Labrador Retriever isn't originally from Labrador at all! The Lab was "discovered" in Newfoundland. In this chapter, you'll also learn about the Labrador Retriever's unique history and how this breed developed from dogs brought to the New World by fishermen. You'll learn a little about his close cousin, the Newfoundland, and how these dogs share the same heritage.

The Chemistry of Labs—Why Labradors Are So Dog-Gone Popular

The Labrador Retriever is the ubiquitous large dog in today's society. Leading in popularity over any other breed, the Lab epitomizes the do-it-all nature. Eager to please, friendly and outgoing, and easily trained, the Lab has captured America's heart.

Lab Lingo

American Kennel Club (or AKC)—The AKC is the oldest and most respected national kennel club in the United States for the advancement of purebred dogs. The AKC promotes purebred dog sports such as conformation and performance events. The AKC was founded in 1884.

No breed comes close to the Lab in number of registrations. In 2001, Labrador Retrievers topped the AKC's registration list with 165,970 dogs. Compare that with the second-most popular dog, the Golden Retriever, coming in at a mere 62,497 registrations. You'd have to add up all the Golden Retrievers, German Shepherd Dogs, and Dachshunds to come close to the number of Labs registered with the AKC.

(Photo courtesy Canine Companions for Independence)

The versatility and friendliness of the Lab makes it an ideal companion as both a pet and a willing worker.

With these numbers, you're probably already familiar with Labs. Your neighbor or friend might have one. You've already been won over by their easy-going temperament and friendliness. Perhaps you think a Lab would be a great pet for your family.

But why are Labs so dog-gone popular? Quite simple: Their personality, their versatility, their trainability, their easy upkeep, and their size make them a winning combination in both home and working environments.

Lab Facts

The Labrador Retriever Club was organized in the United States. in 1931. This club is an official member of the AKC.

Personality Plus—the Successful Experiment

Labs are well known for their easygoing temperament. Labs make great pets for a family that has the time to devote to one. They're people dogs. They can be active, especially dogs who come from hunting lines, but many make fine family pets. Most are good with kids and other pets, including cats—if properly introduced.

Labs are very trainable. As a hunting and water dog, the Lab had to *mark* (note) where the bird fell and then retrieve it on command. This work required a hunting partner who could work without a leash and be reliable, plus retrieve the night's dinner without damaging it. Nowadays, the Lab is superb at obedience, agility, and other competitions.

Lab Lingo

Standard—When talking about dogs, a *standard* is a kind of blueprint for the breed. We say a dog *conforms to the standard* when he meets the size, appearance, movement, and temperament requirements set by the AKC for that breed.

Conformation—The structure of the dog as it conforms to the breed standard.

Mark—To note where a bird has fallen after being shot.

Labs are the quintessential "wash and wear" dogs. Grooming is a breeze because a Lab's coat is short, straight, and sheds water. Labradors do have a thick undercoat, which protects them from the weather. Labs do shed, though, so they need a good brushing once a week and baths when they're dirty. No clipping or trimming is required, however.

Labs are big dogs—something many people like when looking for a pet. Yet, although they are big, they're very adaptable to home environments, provided that they get enough exercise. You'll find Labs in the big cities, in the country, and in the suburbs.

What will you get when you bring a Lab into your home? You'll get the following:

- A companion who is enthusiastic and eager to please.
- A pal who is eager to see you and happy to enjoy your company.
- A willing and tireless worker.

Lab Facts

Labs love carrying around tennis balls and other items. Always have a toy available to play with your Lab.

These are generalizations, however; individual dogs may differ greatly in personality. Because Labs are so popular, many disreputable breeders are producing Labs with health and personality problems, so you must be careful where you get your new pet (see "Reputable Breeders" in Chapter 2 for more information).

Lab Work—What It Means to Bring a Labrador Retriever into Your Life

Now that I've extolled the virtues of the Lab, you might think that it's the most perfect dog in the world. Well, a lot of Lab owners sure think so! But there are downsides to owning a Lab: They are big, strong, and sometimes rambunctious; they need a lot of exercise; and they eat a lot of food. However, many Labrador Retriever owners find that the positives far outweigh the negatives. Many Lab owners are active and enjoy having pets who are so versatile and can enjoy their company in many of their activities.

Large and In Charge

Labs are big, active dogs. Most require a moderate amount of vigorous exercise daily. This includes playing fetch, walks, swimming, and other exercise. Labs can be rambunctious, especially when young. They are strong—so strong that if you don't train one properly, you're likely to go on a "drag" rather than a walk. They can be the proverbial "bull in a china shop" if their owners fail to exercise and train them. Labs are certainly not for everyone; elderly people who can't physically handle a big dog might want to consider a dog that is less physically active.

Lab Bites

Never leave a child alone with a dog, especially an infant or toddler. Dogs can be unpredictable, and even a Lab with the best temperament may bite, especially if he's teased or in pain. Although Labs are considered to be good with kids, always supervise your kids when they're playing with your Lab.

Although standard Labs weigh between 55 and 80 pounds, some dogs may actually be larger than that and may be too much for some people to handle. Can you handle a large, boisterous dog? When young, a Lab may accidentally knock over items either by jumping up or with a sweep of his tail. Lab tails are thick, very strong, and capable of bruising you if you're slapped with them.

Retriever Rewards

Exercise your Lab to help keep him fit, but also to reduce stress and destructive behavior.

Labs can become destructive, especially if left alone for long periods of time. If you don't have the time to spend with your Lab every day, perhaps you should consider a pet who requires less time.

Exercise and Diet

You'll need a fenced-in yard or a kennel if you live in the suburbs or the country. Although you can train your Lab to be fairly reliable when he's off the leash, you should never leave him loose and unsupervised. Many dogs—including Labs—are hit by cars (including, sadly, former President Bill Clinton's Lab, Buddy). If you live in the city, you must walk your Lab several times a day and clean up after him. And you need take your Lab for a long walk every day or play fetch in the park so that he gets his exercise and works off some of that high energy.

Labs eat a lot compared to smaller pets. A Lab may eat a 40-pound bag or more of dog food in a month. Likewise, because they eat more, you'll have more to clean up later.

Lab Tests—the Do-It-All Dog

Labs are the quintessential do-it-all dogs. Whether it's hunting, service work, therapy, or search-and-rescue, Labs dominate. Their good nature and willingness to please and work with their owners make Labs the perfect workers.

Surprisingly, Labs don't necessarily win top awards in obedience competitions—although Labs do well enough. It may be because Labs and their owners are so busy with other pursuits that they don't have an overwhelming desire to become obedience champions.

Lab Facts

Over the years, Labrador Retrievers have separated into Field lines (those used for hunting) and Show lines (those used for showing in competitions). These dogs look different from each other, and there is some friction between the two camps.

Show and Field

As their name suggests, Labs are outstanding retrievers. The AKC offers both field trials and hunting tests for Labrador Retrievers. Your Lab can earn titles in hunting tests such as Junior Hunter, Senior Hunter, or Master Hunter. If you're really competitive, you might want to consider field trials, where your Lab can become a Field Trial Champion (FC). Most people work their Labs in hunting tests. Field tests are much more difficult.

A Comforting Friend—Therapy and Assistance

Labs excel as both therapy and assistance dogs. Their size and demeanor makes them useful for helping their owners, because they are not as intimidating as other large breeds such as German Shepherd Dogs or Rottweilers. Because Labs aren't aggressive and are adaptable to various situations, they are ideal for working around people and encountering new situations.

Therapy dogs are used primarily for visiting hospitals, nursing homes, and schools. These dogs provide comfort and companionship for the sick, disabled, and elderly. Assistance dogs are used for a variety of situations including being used as Seeing-Eye dogs and helping disabled persons fetch and retrieve things, turn on lights, or even help with routine tasks able-bodied people take for granted.

Labs can be independent thinkers. This is crucial in situations that may require quick thinking—such as the need to disobey a command that might jeopardize the owner's life.

(Photo courtesy Canine Companions for Independence)

Because of their temperament and size, Labs are perfect for assistance and therapy work.

Extracurricular Labs—Work in Police, Rescue, and Other Crucial Roles

Labs excel in search-and-rescue and in anything that requires a nose—Labs work as bomb-sniffing, narcotics, and arson dogs. Labs were among the ranks of the search-and-rescue dogs that looked for people trapped in the World Trade Center rubble.

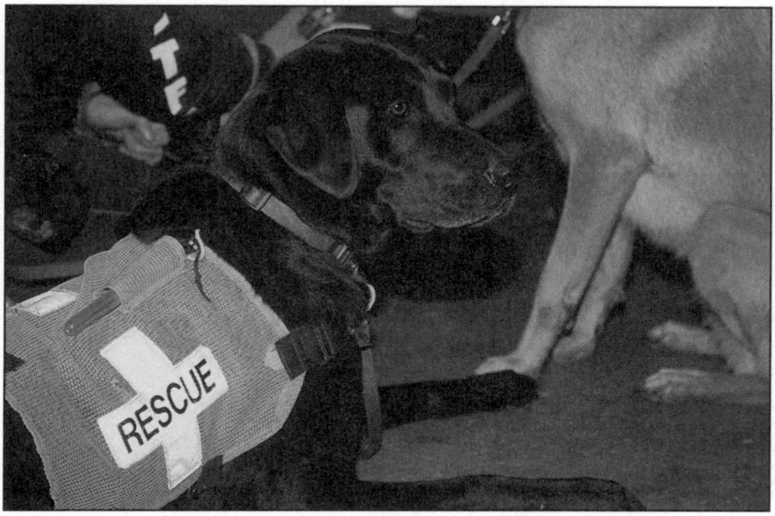

(© Kent and Donna Dannen)

Labs excel in search-and-rescue work.

Retrieving Fame—Lab Celebrities

Not surprisingly, Lab celebrities abound. Many are heroes, in many cases saving their owners from certain death. Some are famous because of their owners or because of their accomplishments.

Hero Labs

Labradors have been awarded the Ken-L Ration Hero of the Year award three times:

- In 1982, Bo rescued his owner from a capsized raft along the Colorado River.
- In 1992, Sparky saved his owner by dragging him over 200 yards to their home after his owner suffered a massive heart attack.

- In 1995, Bailey attacked a 2000-pound bull that pinned his owner and distracted the bull long enough for his owner to escape.

> **Lab Facts**
> Labs played a crucial role in search-and-rescue after the 2001 terrorist attack on the World Trade Center.

Other heroes include Sirius, the canine partner of a Port Authority police officer who tragically died in the World Trade Center's collapse, and the countless dogs who searched for survivors.

Other Notable Labs

- Adjutant was a Black Labrador who is credited by the Guinness Book of World Records as being the world's oldest Lab at 27 years and 3 months.
- Bob in *Watership Down* by Richard Adams was a Black Lab.
- "Boomer" in the movie *Independence Day* (1996) was a Yellow Lab.
- Buddy earned fame and attention as former President Clinton's Chocolate Labrador Retriever.
- "Earl" in the movie *City of Angels* (1998) was a Labrador Retriever.

> **Lab Facts**
> Ch. Boli of Blake was the first Labrador to earn an AKC Champion title, in 1933. (The "Ch." abbreviation before the dog's name stands for "Champion.")

- "Luath" in the movie *The Incredible Journey* (1963) was a Yellow Labrador Retriever.
- "Sam" in the TV show *Sam* (1978) was a Yellow Lab.
- "Sarah" is the Black Labrador host of *Three Dog Bakery* on the Food Network.

500 Years of Labs—a Short History of America's Favorite Dog

No one is certain how the Labrador Retriever first arrived in Newfoundland—or Labrador, for that matter. But most canine historians agree that the Labrador originated in Newfoundland. Newfoundland, off the east coast of Canada, was first settled by Inuits (Eskimos), who had no dogs with them.

In 1494, British traders "discovered" Newfoundland. For the next several centuries, fishermen used Newfoundland as both a home and a port. No doubt, these fishermen brought with them dogs who could hunt and retrieve. These dogs had to be hardy to survive the extreme temperatures and the cold water.

Two types of dogs were prevalent in Newfoundland—one, a large, long-haired dog known as the St. John's Dog or Newfoundland; and another, smaller dog with shorter hair, called the "lesser Newfoundland" or "lesser St. John's Dog." Inhabitants of Newfoundland used the "lesser St. John's Dog" for hunting and retrieving fish and game.

Like its larger cousin, the "lesser" dog was as comfortable in the water as outside of it. Its coat was short and harsh, but underneath sported a downy undercoat to protect it against the cold. Its naturally oily coat repelled water, making it an ideal water dog. These dogs rode in boats and helped their masters while shore fishing, retrieving lines and nets. They had the en-durance to work long hours.

Writings as early as the mid-1600s describe a retriever and hunting dog very similar to the Labrador of today. No doubt these dogs came from the original stock that came with the fishermen in the centuries before this.

Lab Lingo

Retriever—A type of dog used to retrieve game. Labradors are one type of Retriever recognized by the AKC.

A Mystery in History—Why Aren't Labs Called Newfoundland Retrievers?

So, if Labrador Retrievers come from Newfoundland, why aren't they called Newfoundland Retrievers? That's a good question. The Lab was known by several names, including St. John's Dog, lesser St. John's Dog, Newfoundland, and even Labrador.

> **Lab Facts**
>
> The origin of the Labrador Retriever's name dates back to an 1887 letter by the Earl of Malmesbury, in which he mentioned that he always called his retriever dogs "Labrador dogs."

The Third Earl of Malmesbury is reputed to have fixed the name of the Labrador eternally in a letter in 1887, stating "We always called mine Labrador Dog, and I have kept the breed as pure as I could from the first I had …." The name stuck, and as they say, the rest is history.

Tally Ho! To England We Go!

The English hunters and sportsmen quickly took note of the Labrador Retriever. Hunting was popular in the eighteenth and nineteenth centuries among the aristocrats and nobles of England. Nobles such as the Second and Third Earls of Malmesbury, the Fifth and Sixth Dukes of Buccleuch, and the Tenth Earl of Home imported and bred Labradors for hunting and retrieving.

The Labrador Retriever was recognized as a breed by the Kennel Club in England in 1903. Sadly, the Labrador Retriever disappeared in Newfoundland because of a high dog tax. But the breed continued to grow in popularity elsewhere as retrievers and hunters.

Back to America

American sportsmen were quick to notice the Labrador in Britain. In 1917, the first Labrador, Brocklehirst Floss, a female imported from Scotland, was registered with the AKC. The winning personality and versatility of the Labrador soon made it popular among sportsmen. In the 1920s and 1930s, Americans imported many British and Scottish Labs.

(© Katherine Shaver)

The Labrador Retriever is an all-American favorite.

The Lab has since become a popular dog, not only for hunting and retrieving, but for companionship, assistance, and police work. No wonder the Lab is a do-it-all-dog!

Lab Facts

The only accepted colors in Labs are yellow, black, and chocolate. However, "white" and "fox-red" are considered variations of yellow.

Lab Lingo

Show quality—A show-quality puppy or dog is a dog that conforms closely to the standard and may be competitive in a conformation (dog) show.

Pet quality—A pet-quality puppy or dog is a dog that has a superficial blemish or "fault" that would prevent the dog from competing in the conformation (dog) show ring.

The Least You Need to Know

- Labrador Retrievers are the most popular dogs in America and are number one in registrations with the American Kennel Club.
- Labs are known for good temperament and trainability, provided that they come from a reputable source.
- Before you buy a Lab, be certain that you can handle a big dog of 55 to 80 pounds or more, that you have a fenced-in yard for your dog, and that you can exercise him every day.
- Labs excel in search-and-rescue, police work, therapy, and assistance dog work.
- TV and movies are filled with images of hero and celebrity Labs.
- Labrador Retrievers are an old breed dating back to the seventeenth century in Newfoundland. They have also been known as the St. John's Dog, the lesser St. John's Dog, and the Newfoundland.

Chapter 2

Looking for the Right Lab

In This Chapter

- Deciding whether a Lab fits into your lifestyle
- Where you can purchase a quality Lab puppy
- Finding the right Lab for you
- Introducing kids and dogs
- The multiple-animal household

You're thinking about purchasing a Labrador Retriever, but are you sure you're ready for the responsibility? Puppies take time to raise and train. Start preparing for your new dog now by making the right decisions up front. Do you want a puppy or an adult? Should your dog be working, pet, or show quality? Should you buy from a breeder or adopt from a shelter or rescue volunteer?

In this chapter, we'll look into the process of selecting your Labrador Retriever. You'll learn whether a puppy or adult is better for your lifestyle, or whether you might be better off with just a houseplant. We'll look at how kids and dogs get along, and also whether you should get two Labs to keep each other company.

We'll also look at your other pets—if you have them. Are they compatible with a Lab?

(© Jacky Sachs)

Puppies are adorable and Lab puppies are no exception. But be certain that you have the patience and time commitment for a puppy. This is Rosco.

Ir-retrieve-able Consequences—Why Doing Your "Lab Work" Is Important

It's important for you to decide whether or not a Lab will fit into your busy lifestyle now, *before* you purchase a puppy or an adult. Dogs, even the easygoing Lab, are a time commitment. Puppies are worse time-hogs, requiring constant attention, house-training (they don't come pre-housebroken), and obedience training. If you don't have a single minute to yourself now, how are you going to have time for a pet? Consider these facts:

- **A healthy Labrador will live on average 10 to 15 years.** Are you willing to rearrange your lifestyle to accommodate an animal who is dependant solely on you?
- **The cost of a puppy does not end at its purchase price.** Your Lab will require ongoing food and veterinary expenses throughout its entire life. Puppies and elderly dogs generally incur more expenses than adults. Are you financially able to care for your pet?
- **Does everyone in the household want a Labrador or a dog?** All members of the family must agree on a new pet.
- **Is anyone in your house allergic to dogs?** If their allergies aren't manageable, maybe you shouldn't consider owning a dog.
- **Who will take care of the dog?** Children cannot be depended on to take care of a living, breathing animal. The Lab must be the responsibility of an adult in the household.

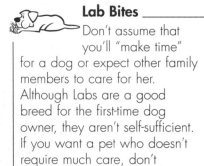

> **Lab Bites**
>
> Don't assume that you'll "make time" for a dog or expect other family members to care for her. Although Labs are a good breed for the first-time dog owner, they aren't self-sufficient. If you want a pet who doesn't require much care, don't choose a dog.

- **Do you have a fenced-in yard that is dig-proof, climb-proof, and jump-proof?**
- **Are you willing to take your Lab for a daily walk or other exercise?** Labs are active dogs.
- **Are you willing to go to obedience classes to train and socialize a puppy?**
- **Are you able to leave your Lab alone for no longer than nine hours?**

- **Are you able to give your Lab attention *every day*?**
- **Are you willing to put up with muddy paw prints on your clothing and carpets?**
- **Can you tolerate hair on your clothes, on your furniture, and in your carpets?** Dog hair has been known to be the fifth food group at my house. Yes, it's everywhere!
- **Are you able to tolerate the destructiveness associated with a dog?** Puppies and dogs may chew the wrong things or dig in the yard. Puppies don't come housebroken and the adult dog may have an occasional accident.
- **Are you willing to clean up after your Lab?** You have to clean up poop piles from your yard and pick up after your dog when you walk him. Sometimes your Lab will get sick and you will have to pick up after he has vomited or has had diarrhea.

If you can truthfully answer each of these questions positively, then you are ready to purchase your Labrador Retriever.

(© Katherine Shaver)

Decide up front what you intend to do with your Retriever, whether it's conformation, hunting, obedience, or just a pet. This is Whooplass Henry Higgins.

Retriever Rewards

Decide up front what you intend to do with your Retriever, whether it's conformation shows, hunting, obedience trials, or just a pet. That will help you determine where to look for your new Lab. Do your research now. A breeder who produces great working Retrievers may not have winners in the conformation show ring.

Lab Legwork: Where (and Where Not) to Get Your Lab

So where should you purchase your Lab? There are good places to purchase a healthy Lab, but there are also many less savory places as well, such as puppy mills and backyard breeders who charge a fair amount for a substandard dog.

Puppy Mills

It's generally a good idea to stay away from any place that produces a high number of puppies. Reputable breeders and dog rescuers call these places "puppy mills" because they constantly churn out puppies for profit. A puppy mill usually has several different breeds, but may have just one. The conditions in many puppy mills are substandard. Puppy bitches are frequently bred during their first heat (at six to eight months) and are bred each subsequent heat cycle thereafter. Some are kept in small, filthy kennels. Puppies are often taken away from their mothers too young and are poorly socialized. Puppies from these conditions are frequently wormy and have external parasites. Their parents were never screened for genetic diseases. No thought is given toward bettering the breed. The dogs are not bred

Lab Facts

The AKC recognizes five Retrievers: the Chesapeake Bay Retriever, the Curly-Coated Retriever, the Flat-Coated Retriever, the Golden Retriever, and the Labrador Retriever.

to the standard; therefore, quite often you will find dogs who vary vastly from dogs seen at shows. The intent of all puppy mills is to produce a profit, not a quality dog.

Given that, do you want to contribute to this market? Buying a Lab puppy from these conditions saves that puppy, but it also provides a market for these unethical breeders. These breeders will continue as long as there is someone willing to buy from them. You can often buy a Lab puppy from a reputable breeder for about the same price or a little more than what you would pay at a puppy mill.

While not all puppy mills are squalid, many are. Some may disguise themselves as reputable breeders. When you see an ad for Labs that advertises "Puppies Always Available," chances are great that it's a puppy mill. Reputable breeders seldom breed more than two litters a year. Some puppy mills, if they offer a guarantee, may impose conditions that are difficult to meet, such as feeding the puppy unusual diets or severely limiting the puppy's exercise.

Backyard Breeders

What about the backyard breeder? This is most likely the first time he's bred his two Labs. He didn't neuter them. He purchased them from a puppy mill or another backyard breeder because he thinks that the word "purebred" means "valuable." He might want to recoup the high price he paid for his dogs. He might have lost the papers a long time ago, or maybe he bred his bitch to his neighbor's Lab who has no papers. It doesn't matter; they're purebred, right? "Hips checked" means he asked the veterinarian if his Labs' hips looked okay. He saw the high prices people sell dogs for in the newspaper, so he thought he can sell them at the same price. The problem is that he has competition for his substandard dogs. The pups are now six weeks old and he didn't realize how expensive and time-consuming they would be to raise. His wife is mad because he hasn't sold the puppies yet and they've become active. They've climbed out of the whelping box and into everything—and they aren't housebroken. He'll sell one to you at a real bargain.

But is it a bargain? Although this fellow is well intentioned, he doesn't know what his puppies will be like. He hasn't chosen the parents based on the standard, so his puppies may look very different than what you might expect. If he bred his Lab to a dog without papers, the puppies might not even be purebred Labrador Retrievers. His puppies could have hip or elbow dysplasia, eye problems, or other diseases. He hasn't vaccinated the pups, nor has he wormed them. He doesn't know much beyond the puppies' parents. He won't offer a guarantee, and he certainly won't take a puppy back.

Lab Bites

Almost all breeds now have genetic problems such as hip dysplasia and progressive retinal atrophy (PRA). Puppy mills and backyard breeders may tell you that they don't need to screen for hip dysplasia and eye problems because genetic diseases are rare in Labs.

Don't believe it. Puppy mills and backyard breeders seldom screen for these diseases. Don't accept statements such as "he's had his hips and eyes checked" or "he doesn't have any genetic diseases." Ask for proof.

Reputable Breeders

I'll be talking a lot about reputable breeders in this and the following chapters. If you are planning to purchase a Labrador Retriever, you're going to be spending a fair amount of money. One look in the newspaper will confirm that. But before you start answering newspaper ads, cruising the mall pet shops, or going over to your neighbor's house to look at the new litter, ask yourself how these people can guarantee the health of their puppies.

Reputable breeders are sometimes called *hobbyist breeders*. That means they aren't breeding dogs specifically for the money. Instead, they're looking to produce top show and working dogs and are trying to improve the breed. These breeders certify that the puppies' parents are free from genetic diseases such as *hip dysplasia* and *progressive retinal atrophy.* These breeders will have you sign a contract and even stipulate that if you have to get rid of your dog for any reason, you will call them first and they will take it back. They stand behind the dogs they produce.

If you are planning to buy a Labrador Retriever, you should buy your Lab only from a reputable breeder. Purchasing your dog from other sources encourages them to continue breeding substandard dogs. See Chapter 3 for more on finding a reputable breeder.

Lab Lingo

Hobbyist breeders—Another name for reputable breeders.

Hip dysplasia—A crippling hereditary disease. This is a prevalent condition among many breeds, including Labrador Retrievers. The hip socket is malformed and the ball and socket that make up the hip don't fit properly, causing limping and great pain. Severe cases of hip dysplasia require expensive surgery that can cost thousands of dollars. Extreme cases of hip dysplasia may require euthanasia.

Progressive retinal atrophy—A genetic eye condition that leads to blindness.

Gimme Shelter

Another place to find a Labrador Retriever is at the local animal shelter or "pound." You might be surprised to hear that one out of four dogs at the pound are purebred and many are Labs. Approximately five million pets fill local shelters and rescues annually, including many young Labs who didn't quite fit for whatever reason.

There are positives and negatives to adopting a dog at the shelter. The biggest negative is that quite often you don't know the dog's history. The dog may have an unseen hereditary medical condition that may show up later. The dog may have learned bad habits from owners who didn't take the time to properly train the dog. Lastly, you usually must spay or neuter a dog from a shelter or rescue, and most dogs coming from shelters don't have their papers anyway. This is not a place to find a conformation champion; however, the AKC will issue ILP (Indefinite Listing Privileges) numbers for dogs who look purebred. ILP dogs can compete in obedience competitions, agility trials, and other sports. (See Chapter 11 for more about dog competitions.)

The positives of adopting a pound dog or puppy are overwhelming. For one thing, you've saved a life and made space for another unwanted pet to have a chance at a new home. Older dogs are usually house trained or can be housebroken more easily than puppies. Older dogs can bond just as closely to their new owners as puppies, so don't discount an older dog because you're afraid he won't bond to you. What's more, now you have an adult dog who you can train in retrieving, agility, or other activities that puppies can't participate in until they're fully grown.

If you do have your heart set on a puppy, sometimes there are purebred Lab puppies available at the pound. Many are older, but a few are from litters from backyard breeders who thought they could make a quick buck breeding their Lab and found that no one wanted their substandard dogs for free, let alone at a price.

Lab Fans to the Rescue

Another place for finding Labrador Retrievers is through Lab rescue. These folks are volunteers who work to place unwanted Labs in good homes. Like reputable breeders, Lab rescue screens its applicants. They may place dogs from shelters, dogs from reputable breeders whose owners returned them, or dogs seized from puppy mills. Sometimes Lab rescue knows the history of the dogs and puppies they place. Some may actually have papers to go along with the dog. These people may or may not be affiliated with the local Lab club, but rescue dogs on a volunteer basis because they love the breed. They're typically overworked and under-appreciated. You might be able to help out by fostering a dog for a while. In the meantime, you could see whether that Lab is the perfect fit for your family!

Lab Facts

There are four types of AKC registrations available to Labs. The most common is *Full Registration*, which people often call the AKC "Papers." A version of the Full Registration is *Limited Registration*, which prevents registration of puppies from the dog. Breeders use this to enforce spay/neuter contracts. A third registration is the *Litter Registration*—often called "Puppy Papers" or "Blue Slips." This is a temporary registration. The fourth is the Indefinite Listing Privilege or ILP Registration. Owners whose dog's background is unknown, but is obviously purebred, may register their dog to compete in obedience, agility, and other activities, with the exception of conformation. ILP dog owners must show proof of having their dogs spayed or neutered.

Finding Your Type

Finding the right Lab is a bit like finding the right mate. You both need to be compatible in order to make the relationship last. A Labrador Retriever is a 10- to 15-year commitment—do your legwork up front to be certain that you find the right match. Otherwise, your Lab will end up the loser.

There's more to a Lab than just color. A Lab is personality on four feet—just be sure your personality and your new Lab's are compatible. Think about the people you like and dislike. I'm sure there are people you know who are nice enough, but who drive you crazy. Make sure that your new Lab's personality isn't one of those. For example, if you're normally quiet, maybe a boisterous dog isn't for you. Or if you're always on the go, maybe an active Lab will add to the fun. Think about what you want to do with your Lab and look for the right personality.

Puppy or Adult?

Puppies are cute, there's no doubt about it, but they're a lot of work. Every time I get a puppy, I'm reminded of just how much work they can be. When considering whether or not you should get a puppy, consider the following:

- Puppies need training, socialization, and attention.
- Puppies aren't housebroken, which means you have to take the time to housebreak your puppy properly.
- Puppies require a series of vaccinations, check-ups, and a spay or neuter operation when they're old enough.
- Puppies are more active and naturally destructive, especially when teething. Anything is fair game to a puppy, so expect a fair amount of destructive behavior.

However, most people prefer puppies to adults. Puppies are, for the most part, a "clean slate." They haven't learned any bad habits yet. If trained and socialized properly, most well-bred puppies turn into excellent companions. Puppies are also so cute that it's hard to resist one.

If you don't have the time for a puppy, consider an adult dog. The benefits to getting an adult dog are the following:

- Most adults are housebroken.
- Many adults know some obedience commands.
- Many breeders will sell their adult dogs to good homes for a lower price than their puppies. Occasionally, reputable breeders may have an adult available. The Lab might be a show prospect who didn't work out or a return from a previous litter.

However, adult dogs may have learned bad habits from previous owners. In rare instances, some adult dogs may not bond as quickly to new owners as a puppy. You also won't have the fun of seeing your puppy grow into an adult.

Lab Facts

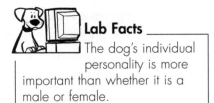

The dog's individual personality is more important than whether it is a male or female.

Whichever you decide, puppy or adult, your new Lab will need training and attention.

Male or Female?

Whether you choose a male or female dog is strictly a personal preference, although there are some differences between the sexes. Note that the following are generalizations and that your Lab's individual personality may override these characteristics:

- Male Labs tend to be more outgoing and boisterous.
- Male Labs may be more apt to challenge your authority than female Labs.
- Males are more dependent on you than females. A male may follow you around more than a female.
- Male Labs tend to be bigger than female Labs.
- Female Labs may be more compliant.
- Female Labs are less likely to challenge you for dominance.
- Female Labs are more independent than their male counterparts.
- Female Labs are generally smaller than males.
- Female Lab go into estrus or "heat" twice a year if they are not spayed. During this time, your Lab will attract male dogs. It is important to keep your female Lab contained safely away from these unwanted suitors during this time.

If you purchase your Lab from a reputable breeder, the breeder may select a puppy for you according to its personality, rather than sex. The puppy's personality is more important than his or her color or sex when determining whether the puppy is in the right home.

Working, Show, or Pet?

What do you intend to do with your Labrador Retriever? Show him in conformation shows ("dog shows")? Work him either in hunting or retriever trials? Or maybe you're just looking for a good all-around pet. Whatever it is, look for the right Lab for the job. Some breeders breed strictly for working or show, but some breed for multiple purposes. Ask.

When you're looking for a Lab for a specific purpose, ask what titles the puppies' parents have obtained (see Chapter 11 for an explanation of the titles Labs can obtain). I've never met a reputable breeder who wasn't delighted to show you photos of the parents, grandparents, and relatives in the working or show environment. Most will haul out stacks of photo albums of their "kids" performing in the field or the ring. You may end up spending hours looking at endless photos of Labs whose names are long and whose titles are even longer! Although you may come out of the session bleary-eyed, you'll know you've found someone whose Labs are their passion and who are very proud of their dogs' accomplishments.

Both show and working lines are fine places to look for pets. But be careful! Some working lines can be more active, due to the energy needed for successful working ability. Talk with breeders to find out if puppies from their lines are more active.

Kids and Dogs

You may have grown up with a dog when you were a kid. Kids and dogs seem to be a natural mix, don't they? Well, sometimes ….

If you have kids, be certain that now is the right time for you to get a dog. A big dog such as a Lab can accidentally injure a toddler or small child by knocking him over or whapping him with its tail. Even an easygoing breed such as the Lab can bite and injure a child if the child handles the puppy roughly or hurts him unintentionally.

Children must learn to respect the puppy as a living, breathing creature. At a young age, it's hard for a child to learn the difference between a puppy and a stuffed toy. Even the most well-intentioned child can hurt a puppy or dog enough to make her bite. For this reason, never leave a child alone with a dog.

Lab Bites

Don't expect your children to take responsibility for your Lab. Even the most responsible kids forget things like letting the dog out or feeding him. Your puppy needs an adult to take responsibility for her welfare. You will be responsible for training, socializing, and caring for your Lab.

The Least You Need to Know

- Before you buy a Lab, you must determine whether this type of dog will fit in with your lifestyle.
- Purchase your Labrador Retriever only from a reputable breeder or adopt from an animal shelter or Labrador Retriever rescue group.
- An adult Lab may be an option if you are too busy to train a puppy, but puppies are less likely to have acquired bad habits and are irresistibly cute.
- Closely monitor children and dogs to make sure they don't accidentally injure one another.

Part 2 Lab Assignments

Congratulations! You've made the decision to bring a Lab into your life. But purchasing or adopting a healthy, well-adjusted Lab takes more than walking over to the local mall or looking through the newspaper. Because Labs are so doggone popular, there are many breeders who breed substandard dogs. These dogs often have genetic diseases such as hip dysplasia that will affect your Lab's health—and your wallet—for years to come.

Part 2 discusses reputable breeders—what makes a reputable breeder and how to find one. I'll also talk about what equipment to purchase and how to puppy-proof or dog-proof your home. I'll talk about how to choose a well-adjusted puppy or adult Lab. Lastly, I'll talk about the first few days with your new addition and about crate training and housetraining.

Chapter 3

Retrieving a Reputable Breeder

In This Chapter

- How do you know a breeder is reputable?
- Finding a reputable breeder
- The health certifications that a reputable breeder should provide for your puppy's parents
- An explanation of all those other papers that come with your puppy
- Is my dog special because he has a pedigree?
- Important points in the breeder contract

You now know that you need to purchase your Lab from a reputable breeder, but how do you go about finding one in the wild? And if you saw one of those rare, elusive creatures, would you recognize one? A reputable breeder screens her dogs for health problems, thus minimizing potential health conditions in the puppies she sells. Puppies aren't always available and she seldom breeds more than two litters a year. Her intent is to improve the breed—not mass-produce puppies.

In this chapter, you'll learn what certifications you should be looking at and what questions to ask. The breeder will also be asking tough questions to be certain that her puppy is going to the best home. You'll learn about AKC papers, contracts, and other useful items. Lastly, you'll learn what clauses are appropriate and not appropriate within the contract.

What's a Reputable Breeder?

What exactly is reputable breeder? A reputable breeder does the following:

- Produces puppies to improve the Labrador Retriever breed.
- Does genetic screening on the parents to minimize the chances that the puppies have hereditary diseases.
- Breeds his dogs infrequently and may have a long waiting list for puppies.
- Carefully screens buyers to make certain that the puppies will have the very best homes.
- Requires spay and neuter contracts for pet-quality puppies.
- Will take back the dog at any time.

This breeder cares about the future of the Labrador Retriever breed and the puppies he brings into this world. He is not breeding Labs to make money, but rather to produce high-quality dogs who will conform to the AKC standard or for working aptitude.

Lab Bites

Avoid purchasing a puppy from any breeder who tries to pressure you into buying one. This breeder isn't interested in producing a quality puppy; this breeder is interested in making money. Reputable breeders don't try to "close the deal."

Always buy from a reputable breeder or adopt a puppy from the shelter or Lab rescue. Quite often puppies from reputable breeders cost the same as puppies from backyard breeders or puppy mills. When you purchase a puppy from a reputable breeder, you purchase a puppy with a known history. The breeder will offer you help and advice in training issues and will take an active interest in your pet. You are not "on your own" if you have training difficulties.

Why Buy from a Reputable Breeder?

Why should you buy from a reputable breeder when there are thousands of puppies available from other sources? First, by purchasing a puppy from other sources, you will be encouraging these sources to continue to breed substandard dogs. These dogs frequently contribute to the pet overpopulation and end up in shelters. The shelters have many Labs and Lab mixes. Second, these sources seldom test the parents for devastating genetic diseases and seldom guarantee their puppies. If they do guarantee the puppy, that guarantee is only as good as the seller. Often, the seller requires that you return the puppy for a refund—little consolation when you have grown attached to your puppy.

(Photo courtesy Canine Companions for Independence)

Always purchase your Lab puppy from a reputable breeder.

Nature *and* Nurture—Reputable Breeder = Healthy Pups

Because reputable breeders care so much for their Labs, they consider their dogs and their puppies members of the family. These breeders raise their puppies in a caring and nurturing environment. They're properly socialized.

A reputable breeder is an expert on dog care. He or she will deworm and vaccinate the puppies to maintain their health. Reputable breeders know how important it is for the puppy to stay with Mom until he is eight weeks old.

Reputable breeders screen for genetic diseases. You have a much better chance at having a healthy, well-adjusted pet than you would from other sources. Quite often, you don't pay more for a puppy from a reputable breeder.

Lab Facts

Ask to see proof of the parents' OFA and CERF certifications. The parents should be certified as clear of hip dysplasia through OFA, Wind-Morgan, or PennHIP, and their eyes should be cleared by CERF.

Although no one can predict the future, most reputable breeders will stake their reputation on their puppies. Occasionally, genetics and other factors come into play and you'll find a sick puppy from a reputable breeder, but the breeder is willing to make amends at that point by either replacing the puppy or offering a refund.

Spotting the Reputable Breeder in the Wild

So, you want to find a reputable breeder, but it's not clear where you should start looking for one. The best place to start is with the Labrador Retriever Club. They have a breeder referral program that will put you in touch with a breeder who is affiliated with the club.

But your work doesn't end there. You still have to grill the breeder to determine whether he or she is reputable. Don't worry!

Reputable breeders won't be put off by your questions—they'll welcome the chance to educate you about themselves and the Labrador Retriever breed. Here are some questions you should ask the breeder:

- **Does the breeder belong to the Labrador Retriever Club or to a local club?**
- **How long has the breeder been involved with Labs?** Backyard breeders are usually new at breeding Labs. Occasionally, you will find a reputable breeder who has just had his first litter, but he is usually also very involved in showing Labs.
- **Does the breeder have only one or two breeds that she breeds?** Reputable breeders focus on one or two breeds to improve the standard.
- **Do the puppies' parents have conformation, obedience, hunting, or agility titles?** A quality Lab should have or be working toward a title. If the parents are not titled, how close are they to obtaining titles?
- **How did the breeder choose the stud dog?** Was the stud a dog the breeder had on hand or did he search for the right dog to breed to his own female? He shouldn't have bred his female to just what was available, but rather, he should have looked for a dog who would improve the conformation and bloodline of his stock.
- **Can she provide photographs and information concerning the parents, grandparents, great-grandparents, uncles, aunts, and cousins of the puppies?** If she cannot tell you about these dogs, how is she able to breed a quality Labrador Retriever?
- **Does the breeder have OFA (or PennHIP or Wind-Morgan) and CERF certification on both parents?**
- **Why did the breeder breed these two Labs?** The answer should be to produce puppies who will improve the Labrador

Retriever breed. Often, the breeder will keep one or two puppies to see if they will turn out to be show prospects. Occasionally, however, the breeder will not keep a puppy because he did not turn out the way the breeder thought he would. Never buy a Lab puppy from someone who is breeding dogs to make a profit. Don't buy a puppy from someone who wanted to breed a Lab just like her pet.

- **A reputable breeder will not press you to buy a puppy.** She will first try to educate you as to what it means to own a Labrador Retriever. She will tell you about the good points and the shortcomings of the breed. She may ask for references. Don't be insulted if she sounds like she is grilling you. She wants to be absolutely certain that this Lab puppy will fit in with your family and your particular situation. If she tells you, "there's only one left, you better buy it"—don't. There are lots of other puppies and other litters from reputable breeders.

Retriever Rewards

Purchasing a puppy from a reputable breeder can be very difficult. However, your work will be well rewarded—you'll have a puppy that is more likely to be healthy and of better temperament than one purchased from a puppy mill, pet shop, or backyard breeder.

- **How old are the puppy's parents?** Neither parent should be bred before two years old. They cannot have their OFA certification until that time.
- **When have the puppies been wormed and vaccinated?** A reputable breeder will either worm the puppies or have a veterinarian perform a fecal analysis on them to determine whether worms are present. Puppies should have received their first vaccinations at five to six weeks of age.
- **When is the earliest the breeder will allow you to take a puppy?** The youngest a puppy should leave his mother is eight

weeks old. *No exceptions.* The puppy must spend time with his mother and littermates to properly socialize him with other dogs. Before this time, the puppy may be very insecure and stunted in his emotional development.

- **What items will the breeder provide when you are ready to take your Lab home?** The breeder should provide you with information on raising and training a Lab, the puppy contract, the AKC puppy papers, copies of the parents' OFA and CERF certifications, a sample of the puppy food she has been feeding the puppies, a record of vaccinations and worming, a vaccination schedule, a pedigree, and any other information she thinks might be useful to a new puppy owner. Some breeders may include a favorite toy to help ease the puppy into his new home.
- **Does the breeder have references?** He should be able to provide you with names and phone numbers of other members of the Labrador Retriever Club or another local club and people who have bought puppies who will gladly vouch for this breeder.

Lab Bites

Be certain your puppy is registered with the American Kennel Club (AKC), the United Kennel Club (UKC), the Canadian Kennel Club, or the FCI (Federacion Cynologique Internacional). In the United States, the main kennel clubs are the AKC and the UKC. Some kennel clubs have been created to legitimize puppy-mill puppies. If you're unsure about a particular kennel club, contact someone from the Labrador Retriever Club and ask.

Health Certifications

Reputable breeders screen for hereditary diseases. Because Labradors are so popular, many are being bred without thought to what genetic diseases they may be passing along to their puppies. These diseases include hip dysplasia (HD), elbow dysplasia (ED), Osteochondritis

Dissecans (OCD), cataracts, progressive retinal atrophy (PRA), central progressive retinal atrophy (CPRA), epilepsy, hypothyroidism, and Tricuspid Valve Dysplasia (TVD).

OFA (or, alternatively, Wind-Morgan or PennHIP) and CERF are two certifications that both of the puppy's parents *must* have. OFA stands for the Orthopedic Foundation for Animals and offers a variety of certifications, including hip, heart, thyroid, and elbow certification. Reputable breeders will minimally have their dogs certified against hip dysplasia. Many will have elbows certified as well because Labradors are prone to elbow dysplasia. Cardiac and thyroid tests further screen out other hereditary diseases. OFA hip and elbow certification lasts for the life of the dog. The following is an example of an OFA health certificate.

Retriever Rewards

Select puppies whose parents' hips were certified OFA GOOD or EXCELLENT only.

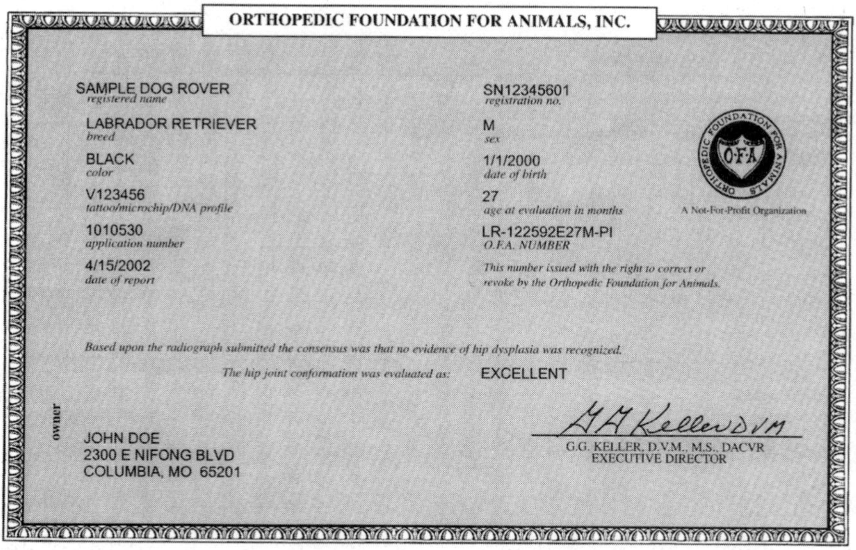

ORTHOPEDIC FOUNDATION FOR ANIMALS, INC.

SAMPLE DOG ROVER
registered name

LABRADOR RETRIEVER
breed

BLACK
color

V123456
tattoo/microchip/DNA profile

1010530
application number

4/15/2002
date of report

SN12345601
registration no.

M
sex

1/1/2000
date of birth

27
age at evaluation in months

LR-122592E27M-PI
O.F.A. NUMBER

This number issued with the right to correct or revoke by the Orthopedic Foundation for Animals.

A Not-For-Profit Organization

Based upon the radiograph submitted the consensus was that no evidence of hip dysplasia was recognized.

The hip joint conformation was evaluated as: EXCELLENT

owner
JOHN DOE
2300 E NIFONG BLVD
COLUMBIA, MO 65201

G.G. KELLER, D.V.M., M.S., DACVR
EXECUTIVE DIRECTOR

The OFA health certificate.

(© The Orthopedic Foundation for Animals)

Lab Bites

Ask to see the *original* health certification documents, not photocopies. Some unscrupulous breeders photocopy the original documents and then write in different dogs' names.

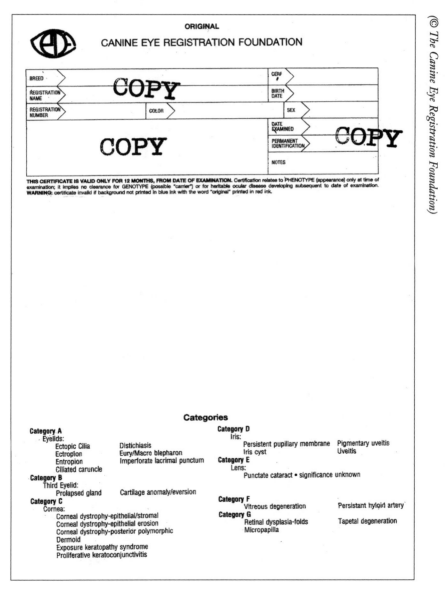

ORIGINAL

CANINE EYE REGISTRATION FOUNDATION

BREED				CERF #	
REGISTRATION NAME	COPY			BIRTH DATE	
REGISTRATION NUMBER		COLOR		SEX	
COPY				DATE EXAMINED	COPY
				PERMANENT IDENTIFICATION	
				NOTES	

THIS CERTIFICATE IS VALID ONLY FOR 12 MONTHS, FROM DATE OF EXAMINATION. Certification relates to PHENOTYPE (appearance) only at time of examination; it implies no clearance for GENOTYPE (possible "carrier") or for heritable ocular disease developing subsequent to date of examination.
WARNING: certificate invalid if background not printed in blue ink with the word "original" printed in red ink.

Categories

Category A
Eyelids:
- Ectopic Cilia
- Ectropion
- Entropion
- Ciliated caruncle
- Distichiasis
- Eury/Macro blepharon
- Imperforate lacrimal punctum

Category B
Third Eyelid:
- Prolapsed gland
- Cartilage anomaly/eversion

Category C
Cornea:
- Corneal dystrophy-epithelial/stromal
- Corneal dystrophy-epithelial erosion
- Corneal dystrophy-posterior polymorphic
- Dermoid
- Exposure keratopathy syndrome
- Proliferative keratoconjunctivitis

Category D
Iris:
- Persistent pupillary membrane
- Iris cyst
- Pigmentary uveitis
- Uveitis

Category E
Lens:
- Punctate cataract • significance unknown

Category F
- Vitreous degeneration
- Persistant hyloid artery

Category G
- Retinal dysplasia-folds
- Micropapilla
- Tapetal degeneration

The CERF health certificate.

The Wind-Morgan Program is a fairly new registry for Labrador Retrievers. This registry is at the University of California at Davis under the Genetic Disease Control Program. Wind-Morgan takes the OFA registry one step further: They evaluate hips, elbows, carpals (wrists), and hocks. The Lab's parents should have either Wind-Morgan or OFA certification.

CERF, or the Canine Eye Registration Foundation, certifies that the dog's eyes are clear of disease. This certification must be updated yearly.

Retriever Rewards

Both OFA and CERF have online databases to search for certified dogs. You can find your prospective puppy's parents by searching the breed and for the dog's registered name—or even part of the dog's registered name—at www.offa.org and www.vmdb.org/cerf.html.

What Are "Papers"?

Your Labrador Retriever puppy should have "papers"—that is, the AKC registration. All purebred AKC dogs have AKC registration. This is the proof that your Lab is a registered purebred. It is *not* a symbol of quality. It does *not* mean that your Lab is somehow very valuable or more valuable than anyone else's is. It does *not* mean your Lab is show quality. It does *not* mean your Lab is healthy or well bred.

Breeders refer to the "puppy papers" as "blue slips." On one, you will find a place to fill in your Lab's name, your name, and a place where both you and the breeder must sign to indicate a transfer of ownership. AKC now has a checkbox that the breeder checks if the puppy will have a limited registration. If this box is checked, the puppy may not ever be bred and cannot have her litters registered under AKC. In this way, a reputable breeder may indicate that the puppy is being sold to a pet home only. Only the breeder may rescind this limited registration. The breeder may opt for a full registration in writing if you request it and he deems the puppy to be show quality. Dogs with limited registration may not be shown in dog shows.

Lab Facts

What does all the mumbo-jumbo around the name mean on a registration? Look at the following example of a fictitious Lab:

DC Sky Warrior's Retrievers Rewards CDX, TD
SH921234 6-01 OFA12G YLW

The dog's registered name is Sky Warrior's Retrievers Rewards. The dog has several titles including Dual Champion (DC), Companion Dog Excellent (CDX), and Tracking Dog (TD).

The number right below the name is the dog's AKC registration number. Right after it is the date—in this case, June 2001—when the dog was registered in the AKC Stud Book—that is, a book maintained by the AKC that lists all dogs who have been bred. The OFA number is the OFA registration, and the letter after the number—G, E, or F—indicates its rating. (In this case—G for Good). Older OFA numbers don't have this rating. Lastly, you see the dog's color—that is, YLW or Yellow.

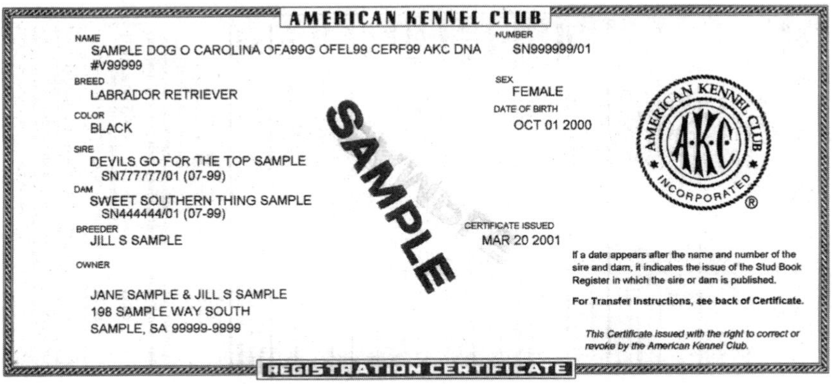

AMERICAN KENNEL CLUB

NAME
SAMPLE DOG O CAROLINA OFA99G OFEL99 CERF99 AKC DNA #V99999

NUMBER
SN999999/01

BREED
LABRADOR RETRIEVER

SEX
FEMALE

COLOR
BLACK

DATE OF BIRTH
OCT 01 2000

SIRE
DEVILS GO FOR THE TOP SAMPLE
SN777777/01 (07-99)

DAM
SWEET SOUTHERN THING SAMPLE
SN444444/01 (07-99)

BREEDER
JILL S SAMPLE

CERTIFICATE ISSUED
MAR 20 2001

OWNER
JANE SAMPLE & JILL S SAMPLE
198 SAMPLE WAY SOUTH
SAMPLE, SA 99999-9999

SAMPLE

AMERICAN KENNEL CLUB INCORPORATED A·K·C ®

If a date appears after the name and number of the sire and dam, it indicates the issue of the Stud Book Register in which the sire or dam is published.

For Transfer Instructions, see back of Certificate.

This Certificate issued with the right to correct or revoke by the American Kennel Club.

REGISTRATION CERTIFICATE

(© The American Kennel Club)

Full Registration certificate.

AMERICAN KENNEL CLUB

NAME
SAMPLE DOG O CAROLINA OFA99G OFEL99 CERF99 AKC DNA #V99999

NUMBER
SN999999/01

OFFSPRING OF THIS DOG NOT ELIGIBLE FOR REGISTRATION

BREED
LABRADOR RETRIEVER

SEX
FEMALE

COLOR
BLACK

DATE OF BIRTH
OCT 01 2000

SIRE
DEVILS GO FOR THE TOP SAMPLE
SN777777/01 (07-99)

DAM
SWEET SOUTHERN THING SAMPLE
SN444444/01 (07-99)

BREEDER
JILL S SAMPLE

CERTIFICATE ISSUED
MAR 20 2001

OWNER
JANE SAMPLE & JILL S SAMPLE
198 SAMPLE WAY SOUTH
SAMPLE, SA 99999-9999

SAMPLE

AMERICAN KENNEL CLUB INCORPORATED AKC ®

If a date appears after the name and number of the sire and dam, it indicates the issue of the Stud Book Register in which the sire or dam is published.

For Transfer Instructions, see back of Certificate.

This Certificate issued with the right to correct or revoke by the American Kennel Club.

LIMITED REGISTRATION CERTIFICATE

Limited Registration certificate.

(© *The American Kennel Club*)

Even if you have "puppy papers" from the breeder, your Lab isn't officially registered with the AKC. You must fill out the appropriate boxes and send the form into AKC along with the registration fee. Don't confuse the pedigree with the registration. The pedigree is the puppy's family tree. It may look very impressive with dogs with strange registered names and the authentic AKC gold seal, but again, it is not a sign of quality nor does it register your puppy to you.

Lab Lingo

Pedigree—A dog's family tree.

Champion—Abbreviated CH. A designation given to a dog who earns 15 points in conformation dog shows, including 3 points or better under two different judges. The number of points earned depends on the region, the breed, and the number of dogs entered.

Field trial champion—Abbreviated FC. A hunting title obtained when the dog wins either a National Championship Stake or 10 points in Open All-Age, Limited All-Age, Special All-Age, or Restricted All-age competition.

Dual champion—Abbreviated DC. A dog who has his CH and his FC titles.

AMERICAN KENNEL CLUB **Dog Registration Application**

Use this form to register your purebred dog with the AKC. Important information and instructions are on the back of this form. Please use black ink and capital letters to fill in the boxes. Information you omit or print outside of the boxes will delay processing. **Registration is not guaranteed. Application fees are nonrefundable and are subject to change without notice.**

Litter Information

Breed	LABRADOR RETRIEVER	Number: SN00000001	
Date of Birth	JANUARY 1 2002		
Sire	MISTER GEORGE SAMPLE DOG SN999999/99 (8-96)	Dam	MADAM JENNY SAMPLE DOG SN888888/88 (5-02)
Breeder	SALLY SAMPLETON		
Litter Owner	SALLY SAMPLETON 123 N SAMPLE STREET SAMPLE, SA 00000-0000		

Optional Registration Packages: costs are in addition to the basic registration fee

☐ Gold Package: $25 (Save $7.95!)
- Dog Care Training Video
- Three Generation AKC Certified Pedigree (traces back three generations of your dog's ancestry)

☐ Silver Package: $17 (Save $3.00!)
- Three Generation AKC Certified Pedigree (traces back three generations of your dog's ancestry)

Note: All items are mailed separately.

Payment Information

Basic registration. Includes an official AKC Registration Certificate. → **AKC Registration** $ 1 5

Enter an additional $25 for the Gold Package or $17 for the Silver Package if applicable. → **Gold or Silver Package** $

Calculate transfer fee and attach a Supplemental Transfer Statement, if applicable. **Number of transfers:** ☐ x $15 → **Transfer Fee** $

Enter $35 if you are submitting this form after APRIL 8, 2003 or $65 if you are submitting it after APRIL 8, 2004. → **Late Fee** $

Total Fee $

Charge my: ☐ VISA ☐ AMEX ☐ MasterCard

Account Number (do not include dashes) Expiration Date Signature of Cardholder

Name of Dog: the registering owner has the right to name the dog

Print one capital letter per box. Skip a box between words. Choose a unique name. Names are subject to AKC approval. Once a dog is registered, its name cannot be changed.

Dog Name

Permission To Use An AKC Registered Kennel Name: required if being used as part of this dog's name

Registered Kennel Name Kennel Name Owner's Signature Customer Number

Check the sex of the dog you are registering

Male ☐ **Female** ☐

Check to request Limited Registration

Limited ☐ The dog is not to be used for breeding. Entry in dog events is restricted.

Color

Enter the 3-digit code for the color that most closely describes your dog.

007 BLACK 071 CHOCOLATE
232 YELLOW

Markings

Enter the 3-digit code for the marking pattern that most closely describes your dog.

SAMPLE

STOP If you are the litter owner(s) and are applying to register this dog, the information you have supplied on this page is sufficient. Otherwise, you must complete the back of this form.

S N 0 0 0 0 0 0 0 1

ADREG2 (03/02) M00F01 © 2002 The American Kennel Club

(© The American Kennel Club)

Dog registration papers, or "blue slips."

AMERICAN KENNEL CLUB **Dog Registration Application**

SN00000001

New Owner Information

I (we) sold this dog **directly** to the owner(s) listed below. Date of Sale: Month – Day – Year

New Owner's First Name | New Owner's Last Name

Check here if the new owner is an Organization | Enter Customer Number, if available

Street Address

City | State | ZIP code + 4

Telephone Number | Email Address

New Co-Owner's First Name | New Co-Owner's Last Name

Check here if the new co-owner is an Organization | Enter Customer Number, if available

Street Address

City | State | ZIP code + 4

Telephone Number | Email Address

SAMPLE

I certify by my signature that all the information appearing on this application is correct and that I am in good standing with The American Kennel Club.

SALLY SAMPLETON

Check One: sign here *only* if you are registering this dog in your name

I (we) apply to the American Kennel Club to have a Registration Certificate for this dog issued in my (our) name(s) and certify that I (we) acquired this dog on the date stated above directly from the Litter Owners. I (we) agree to abide by all rules and regulations of the American Kennel Club. I (we) understand that if the Limited box on the Dog Registration Application has been checked by the Litter Owner(s), I (we) will receive a Limited Registration Certificate.

New Owner's Signature | New Co-Owner's Signature

I (we) transferred ownership of this dog to another person. **A Supplemental Transfer Statement and a $15.00 fee must accompany this application for each intermediate transfer. This dog's registering owner must sign the last such form.**

Instructions, Requirements, and General Information

Mailing/Faxing Information	Send this form and all appropriate fees to: The American Kennel Club, Dog Applications, P.O. Box 37902, Raleigh, NC 27627-7902. If you use a credit card, you may fax one or both sides of this form, as appropriate, to: (919) 816-3627. Please *do not* use a cover sheet.
Additional Requirements	• **If there are more than two (2) owners, contact the AKC for an Additional Signature form.** • **A Supplemental Transfer Statement and a $15.00 fee must accompany this application for *each* intermediate transfer.** **Note:** These forms are available on our web site: www.akc.org.
Authorizations	Signatures of persons other than the owners will be accepted only if a properly completed authorization form has been filed with the AKC. **Note:** These forms are available on our web site: www.akc.org.
Assistance	Email AKC at info@akc.org or call 919-233-9767 to speak to an AKC Customer Service Representative, Monday — Friday, 8:30 AM — 5:00 PM. Information about the registration process and downloadable forms are available on our web site: www.akc.org.
Notice	If this application contains any error or misrepresentation, the AKC may correct or cancel the registration of this dog and its descendents. Misrepresentation may also result in the loss of AKC privileges. Corrections may be cause for rejection or a delay in registration for an explanation. **Registration is not guaranteed. Application fees are nonrefundable and are subject to change without notice.**

ADREG2 (03/02)

Dog registration papers, or "blue slips."

What's a Pedigree?

You may be surprised to learn that all dogs have pedigrees, even the lowly mutt. It's true. In fact, all people and animals have pedigrees. What is a pedigree? It's a family tree—that's all. If you were born, you've got one. Simple, huh?

Is This a Good Pedigree?

In registered dogs, the AKC (or in some cases, the UKC) keeps track of your Lab's pedigree. There's no differentiation between a good pedigree and a bad pedigree when it comes to the registration. That's up to you to figure out. Just because your Lab has an impressive five-generation pedigree doesn't mean that those ancestors were show or field-trial champions. In fact, in many pedigrees you'll see impressive-sounding names, but the dogs were products of puppy mills or worse.

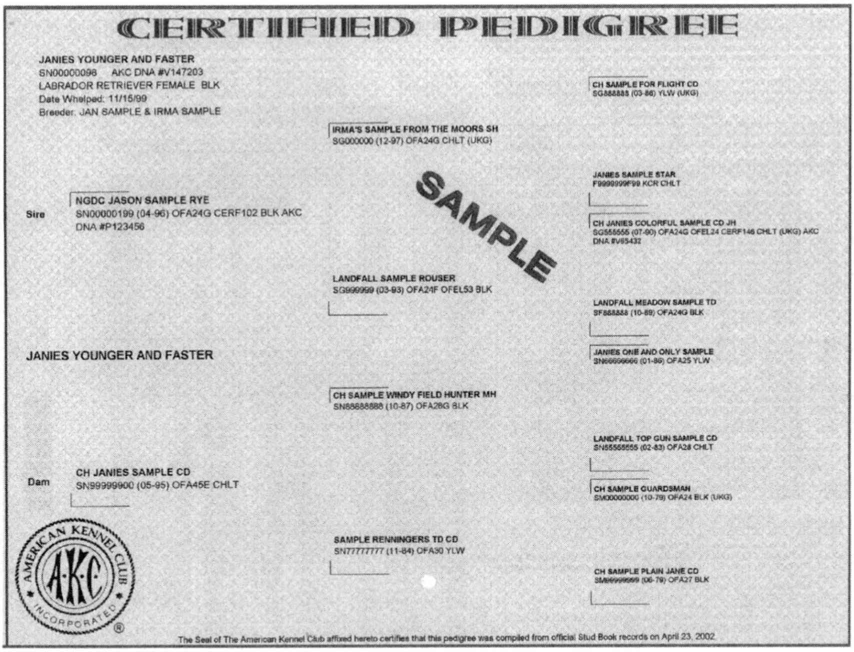
CERTIFIED PEDIGREE

JANIES YOUNGER AND FASTER
SN00000098 AKC DNA #V147203
LABRADOR RETRIEVER FEMALE BLK
Date Whelped: 11/15/99
Breeder: JAN SAMPLE & IRMA SAMPLE

Sire
NGDC JASON SAMPLE RYE
SN00000199 (04-96) OFA24G CERF102 BLK AKC DNA #P123456

IRMA'S SAMPLE FROM THE MOORS SH
SG000000 (12-97) OFA24G CHLT (UKG)

CH SAMPLE FOR FLIGHT CD
SG888888 (03-86) YLW (UKG)

JANIES SAMPLE STAR
F9999999F99 KCR CHLT

CH JANIES COLORFUL SAMPLE CD JH
SG555555 (07-90) OFA24G OFEL24 CERF146 CHLT (UKG) AKC DNA #V65432

SAMPLE

LANDFALL SAMPLE ROUSER
SG999999 (03-93) OFA24F OFEL53 BLK

LANDFALL MEADOW SAMPLE TD
SF888888 (10-89) OFA24G BLK

JANIES ONE AND ONLY SAMPLE
SN66666666 (01-86) OFA25 YLW

JANIES YOUNGER AND FASTER

CH SAMPLE WINDY FIELD HUNTER MH
SN88888888 (10-87) OFA28G BLK

LANDFALL TOP GUN SAMPLE CD
SN55555555 (02-83) OFA28 CHLT

CH SAMPLE GUARDSMAN
SM00000000 (10-79) OFA24 BLK (UKG)

Dam
CH JANIES SAMPLE CD
SN99999900 (05-95) OFA45E CHLT

SAMPLE RENNINGERS TD CD
SN77777777 (11-84) OFA30 YLW

CH SAMPLE PLAIN JANE CD
SM99999999 (06-79) OFA27 BLK

AMERICAN KENNEL CLUB AKC INCORPORATED ®

The Seal of The American Kennel Club affixed hereto certifies that this pedigree was compiled from official Stud Book records on April 23, 2002

(© The American Kennel Club)

An AKC Lab pedigree.

So, how do you tell? First of all, look at the *titles* next to the names. AKC abbreviates titles such as Champion, Field Trial Champion, and Obedience, Agility, and Tracking titles and puts them on the pedigrees.

So, How Do You Read an AKC Pedigree?

It's relatively easy, so to speak. The name, breed, and birth date of the dog appear in the top-left corner. The dog's sex, registration number, color, and breeder are in the upper-right corner.

You read from left to right. The top leftmost is the sire (father); the bottom leftmost is the dam (mother). To the right are four more names. Those are the dog's grandparents. The two topmost are the paternal grandparents; the two bottommost are the maternal grandparents. Males are always on top; females are below. The next row is the great-grandparents, with each grandparent's sire and dam. And so on.

Retriever Rewards

What's in a name? Well, breeders are funny folk and love to give their dogs fun names. That's why you'll see so many weird names on pedigrees. The standard way of naming is the kennel name of the breeder followed by whatever you'd like. It can be your dog's call name, but it doesn't have to be. A friend of mine's dog was named Belle's Cool Holiday Special, but he answered to Buddy!

The Contract

Ask the breeder if he or she has a contract. The contract is your bill of sale. The AKC papers are *not* a bill of sale. If the breeder does not have a contract, look elsewhere. The contract is important because it protects you if something goes wrong. If there is something in the contract that you don't understand, consult a lawyer.

Right of First Refusal

Every reputable breeder has a "Right of First Refusal" or "First Right of Refusal" clause in their contract. This means that the breeder has the option of taking back the dog if you no longer want him. However, be careful if there is only a "Right of First Refusal" in the contract. Some breeders use this clause as a way of looking responsible, but they treat it as an option and won't take back the dog if you can't or won't keep him.

A truly reputable breeder will take the Lab back under any condition and will state so in the contract. That means that three weeks or three years from now, the breeder will take back the Lab if he isn't working out. Most breeders have a limited clause on a refund, so don't expect to get your money back after a year.

Health Guarantee

In the contract, the breeder should also guarantee his puppy to be free from illnesses, parasites, and hereditary defects. Again, most of these guarantees have reasonable time limits. Breeders usually require the owners to take their puppies to the vet within the first week to ensure the puppy's health. Most breeders will replace or refund at the breeder's discretion. This is small consolation if your Lab has hip dysplasia and you are already attached to him. That is why it is very important to do your "lab work" and make certain the breeder has screened for these diseases.

Your Responsibilities Under the Contract

In the contract, a reputable breeder will stipulate that you must adequately care for the puppy and will require that you must never allow your Lab puppy to run at large. The contract should not give the breeder stud rights or state requirements for breeding unless this is something you've agreed with prior to seeing the contract. The guarantee should not have a caveat such as strange diets or extreme limitation of exercise.

If a breeder sells your Lab as a pet-quality dog, you may have a spay/neuter clause in your contract. If you are planning to show your Lab in conformation, request that the breeder remove this clause and explain why. If the puppy isn't show quality, the breeder may suggest another puppy or breeder. Otherwise, if your puppy is intended to be a pet, this is a normal clause and you should spay or neuter the puppy.

Lab Bites

Some disreputable breeders will demand stud rights or have requirements for breeding in their contract. Unless this is something you've agreed with prior to seeing the contract, don't accept it.

Furthermore, some disreputable breeders will guarantee the health of your Lab, but only with extreme conditions such as requiring you to adhere to strange diets or extreme limitation of exercise. Disreputable breeders use these clauses to nullify the contract when you don't follow the conditions.

The Least You Need to Know

- A reputable breeder cares about the breed, does genetic screenings on his dogs, breeds the dogs infrequently, and screens potential buyers.
- You can find a reputable breeder through the Labrador Retriever Club, but you still need to grill the candidates.
- Your new puppy's parents must both have OFA (or, alternatively, Wind-Morgan) and CERF certifications.
- Your puppy should come with AKC registration papers.
- A pedigree is simply your dog's family tree.
- Be certain the breeder has a contract and that it is fair. The contract is your bill of sale.

Chapter 4

Retrieving the Perfect Lab

In This Chapter

- Visiting prospective breeders
- Finding the best Lab puppy for you
- Selecting an adult Lab

You've done your "Lab work" and now is the time to visit prospective breeders and their puppies. How do you select the perfect puppy for you? Personality varies among puppies and you'll want to find the puppy who will fit perfectly into your household.

If you've decided that an adult Lab is more suitable for your lifestyle, you still need to be selective in your search for the perfect canine companion.

Visiting the Breeder

You've done your homework and you're now ready to visit the breeder. If the puppies aren't born yet, the breeder may offer to put you on a waiting list for pups. If the puppies are already born but are still too young to take home, you'll want to see the breeder's kennel anyway. The more you can learn about the breeder and your puppy's background, the better.

Check Out the Facilities and the Dogs

Breeders should be happy to let you visit their kennels. All their dogs should be approachable—even big males. If the breeder tells you that the dog is mean because he's a stud dog, you might want to reconsider purchasing a puppy from her. Only a female with puppies should be protective, but not necessarily aggressive.

(Photo courtesy Canine Companions for Independence)

Do your research to determine whether the puppy you're buying comes from a reputable breeder.

Look around the kennels. Are there several breeds present? Do you see rows and rows of dogs and several litters? Do the dogs look sickly and ill-kept? If so, you may be at a puppy mill. Don't buy a puppy here.

A reputable breeder may have many dogs, but generally focuses on one or two breeds. There aren't rows and rows of puppies to choose from. Instead, this may be the only litter the breeder will breed this year—or within the next two years. The breeder is looking to improve his dogs, *not* to make money.

If the breeder has puppies available, look at the puppies. Healthy puppies are everything you expect them to be: active, healthy-looking, bright-eyed, and full of energy. Sick puppies will cry, appear listless, and have poor hair-coats, runny noses, potbellies, and goopy eyes. Healthy puppies may be inactive when they first wake up, but they should be active once they wake.

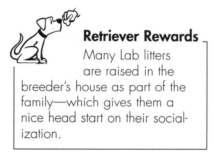

Retriever Rewards

Many Lab litters are raised in the breeder's house as part of the family—which gives them a nice head start on their socialization.

This Might Be the Place

If the puppies are ready to be taken home, no matter how cute they might be, don't buy a puppy right then and there. All Lab puppies are adorable, and the next litter will steal your heart just as easily. Go over the contract, look at the health certifications, and talk with the breeder about what you are looking for in a Lab.

Once you decide on a breeder, let the breeder know. If the puppies aren't born yet or if they aren't old enough to take home, the breeder may request a deposit on one. The amount of the deposit depends on the breeder; it can be anywhere up to one-fourth of the puppy's purchase price. If the puppies aren't born, the breeder should return the deposit. That deposit may reserve a puppy of either sex or a puppy of one or the other sex. Again, that depends on the breeder.

Lab Bites

Don't be too eager to purchase your Lab puppy from the first breeder you visit. Do your homework and research first to determine whether this breeder is breeding quality puppies. Don't allow the breeder to pressure you into buying a puppy.

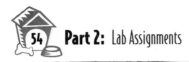

The Pick of the Litter

You may be surprised to learn that many breeders select your puppy for you. They've sized you up and decided which puppy is best for your circumstances. For instance, you may be looking for an enjoyable pet and may be a first-time dog owner. In this case, an overly active puppy may not fit into your lifestyle. A good breeder observes the puppies daily, looking at temperaments and behavior. They also often conduct puppy tests to see which pups fit which lifestyles.

The Puppy Personality Test

Even if the breeder does select your puppy, you may want to test your puppy's personality. If you are looking for a pet, you will want a puppy who is neither too dominant nor too submissive.

When you visit the puppies, call to them. They should come to you readily. The first puppy who greets you may be more dominant, but this depends largely on where the puppies were when you called them. Puppies who visit and then go off may be independent-minded. These free spirits may be difficult to train because they're more interested in their surroundings than you. Likewise, puppies who hang back or act fearful may be too submissive.

Lab Bites

My mom always said "You can't tell a book by its cover." How true with Labs! Don't choose your Lab based on looks or color alone or you may be terribly disappointed. After health, your Lab's personality should be your number-one concern.

Active is good, but hyper is not. Let the puppies calm down a bit and play with them. Puppies who play very aggressively with their siblings or with you may be too dominant. At this point, with the approval of the breeder, separate each of the puppies you're considering from their siblings and play with them.

Most puppies, when separated, may become a little nervous. But as you're playing with them, they will become cheerful and relaxed. Negative reactions include becoming fearful, aggressive, or overly hyper. If the puppy you're thinking of buying exhibits any of these behaviors, look at another puppy.

With the breeder's permission, gently pick up the puppy and cradle him so that he is on his back. Some puppies will become very fearful or will struggle violently. A calm and self-assured puppy will perhaps struggle a little and then relax as you give him a tummy rub. If the puppy reacts very negatively—either fearful or aggressive—put him down.

The Unscientific Eyesight and Hearing Test

Lastly, you'll want to check the puppy's eyesight and hearing. Roll a ball or wave a toy in front of his face to see if he will react. Clap your hands or snap your fingers behind his head to see if he will turn his head and look or at least react. These tests aren't scientific, but they may show if there is an eyesight or hearing problem.

Lab Facts

Dogs, being descended from wolves, have inherited their ancestors' pack behavior. Among wolves and wild dogs, there are certain personalities that predispose dogs to becoming alpha—that is, "top dog." There are alpha personalities in both male and female dogs. Alpha dogs will typically challenge other dogs (and their owners) for the right to be in charge. This is why trainers don't recommend that the inexperienced dog owner get an alpha dog.

Other personalities will also challenge, but to a lesser extent. The very lowest and most submissive in the hierarchy can be just as bad as the alpha dog. These omega dogs frequently become dogs that bite when they are scared if you don't recognize them and properly train and socialize them.

Labs aren't as difficult as some breeds—most notably the independent Nordic breeds and some hound breeds—but as a Lab owner, you must be aware that there is a potential for problems.

When selecting a Lab puppy, you'll be looking for one who isn't too dominant or submissive. This is Whooplass Henry Higgins.

Selecting an Older Dog

Selecting an older dog is a little easier than selecting a puppy. Unlike puppies, the older Lab is basically "what you see is what you get," unless she's just an older puppy. If there is any way for you to find out the older dog's history, do so. Talk with the owner, if you can.

Return to Sender

If the Lab has been returned to the breeder by her first owner, ask the breeder why. If the dog is at a shelter, sometimes a shelter can tell you why the dog is there. Be aware that previous owners often will lie about why the dog is being returned. A typical response is "allergies," so don't always believe that the former owners returned your prospective Lab or dumped him in the shelter because someone suddenly became allergic to them. Many dogs dumped at shelters are young males between 6 and 12 months of age. These are "teenage" dogs; with some time, exercise, consistent training, and attention they will often turn out just wonderful.

Typical reasons people relinquish their pets include the following:

- Behavioral problems (many of which can easily be corrected by someone willing to take the time to do so)
- Inconvenience (the owner didn't have time)
- Lifestyle change (such as a marriage, a new baby, or moving far away or to a place that doesn't allow pets)
- Death of the owner
- Expense (the owner couldn't afford the dog anymore)

Having worked with a variety of rescued dogs, I can state that the former owners caused many of their behavioral problems and that firm, consistent training eliminates most problems. This isn't to say that you won't find a dog that isn't trainable. They're out there, but they're a rarity. Most shelter dogs make sweet pets.

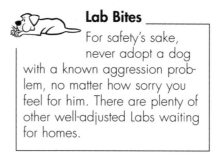

> **Lab Bites**
>
> For safety's sake, never adopt a dog with a known aggression problem, no matter how sorry you feel for him. There are plenty of other well-adjusted Labs waiting for homes.

Checking the Adult Dog's Personality

Meet the Lab in a quiet room if you can. See how the dog reacts toward you. Is he cringing and fearful or friendly and outgoing? It's okay for the dog to show some trepidation followed by cheerful acceptance. If the Lab continues to act fearful or submissive—or act wild and unruly—you probably don't want this Lab. You want a dog who acts friendly.

Next, put the Lab on a leash and walk him. See how he reacts to you. If he knows any commands, work with him on them and see how he reacts. If there is any aggression or questionable behavior, you may want to look elsewhere.

(© Kent and Donna Dannen)

When looking for an adult Lab, look for one with a good temperament.

The Least You Need to Know

- When you visit a potential breeder, learn as much as you can about the breeder's practices and the puppies' backgrounds. Reputable breeders will allow you to meet with all dogs in their kennel.
- Many reputable breeders will have already selected a puppy for you based on the puppy's personality and your lifestyle. If not, choose your Lab puppy on personality, not on looks alone.
- Choose an adult Lab who is friendly and outgoing and responds well to you.

Chapter 5

Retrieving Lab Equipment

In This Chapter

- Selecting the right equipment for your Lab
- Safe and unsafe toys, chews, and bones
- The right food for your Lab

In this chapter, we'll look at the necessary supplies you should buy for your Lab before he comes home, plus those things that make your life that much easier, whether you're bringing home a puppy or an adult. We also focus on safe and unsafe things to chew, as well as selecting the right food for your dog.

Buying Doggie Supplies

Before you bring your Lab home, purchase all the necessary items for your new dog or puppy. If you purchase the equipment now, before you bring your new addition home, you may be able to save both time and money. Don't wait until the last minute! Often you pay more than if you planned ahead, and many times the closest store may not have what you need. Items such as crates and beds, for example, are usually not available at the grocery store.

If you have enough time, you may want to purchase your Lab's supplies from discount catalogues or from the Internet. I like using KV Vet Supply (www.kvvet.com), Drs. Foster and Smith (www.drsfostersmith.com), and RC Steele. These suppliers offer a wider variety than the local pet boutique or even the big pet-supply stores, and often at a substantial discount. Be careful to check the shipping charges—sometimes they add up to more than the discount!

> **Retriever Rewards**
>
> Quite often, you can save money by buying your Lab supplies from discount pet-supply catalogs or over the Internet.

Large pet-supply stores may offer discounted items, or they may be just as expensive as a specialty shop. It depends on the item. It really does pay to comparison shop.

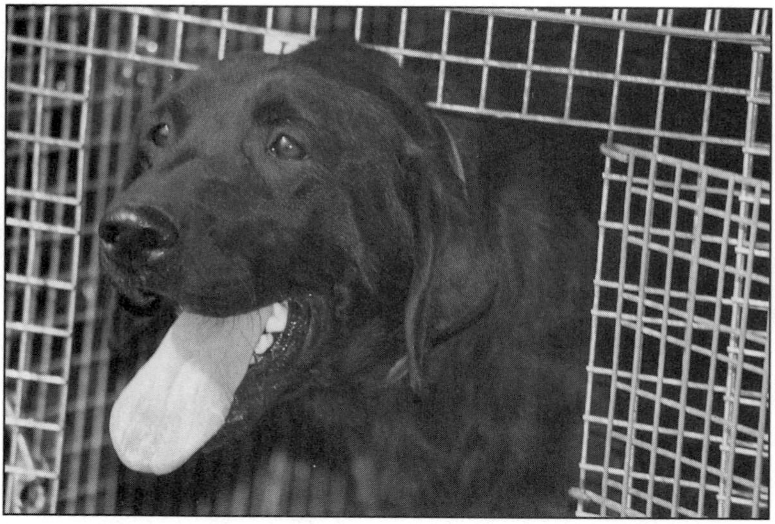

(© Kent and Donna Dannen)

This Lab considers his crate his "den." This is a wire crate.

Must-Have Items

But, what does your Lab really need? The basics include the following:

- A training crate. Needs to be large enough for an adult Lab to stand up, lie down, and turn around comfortably. Some owners like to purchase a puppy crate, and then as the puppy grows bigger, purchase a crate for an adult. Puppy crates are usually cheaper with lighter-gauge wire.

Crates come in three types. One is the wire mesh type. The second is the travel crate, approved for airline use. Both have their advantages and disadvantages. The wire mesh type allows more air circulation. You can use the travel crate for airline travel (provided it is approved for that). The third is a relatively new type of crate that is collapsible and made from fabric. These crates are intended for traveling and obedience-trained dogs who are already crate-trained. Do not purchase this type of crate for a puppy or an adult as a permanent crate.

Lab Facts

Crates are not cages! To your Labrador Retriever, a crate is a safe haven away from the hustle and bustle of the household. Because dogs are descendants of wolves, they've inherited the wolf's denning instinct. Your Lab will look on his crate as his safe place.

- Bed or bedding material (should fit in the crate).
- Fencing or some other containment system for outdoors.
- Water and food bowls.
- Premium puppy or dog food (more about this in a later section).
- Flat collar or buckle collar (for everyday wear and identification).
- Identification tags.
- Training collar.
- Six-foot leather leash.
- Enzymatic cleaner for accidents.

Retriever Rewards

You don't have to mail away for ID tags. Often, large pet-supply stores have machines that engrave identification tags right in the store. So, you can pick up your Lab's ID tag while you're shopping for dog food and pet supplies! They cost around $4 to $6.

- Slicker brush (wire brush) and comb.
- Doggie nail clippers.
- Doggie toothbrush and toothpaste—not the human kind!
- Doggie shampoo—not human shampoo!
- Puppy/training treats.
- Suitable toys and chewing objects.

Lab Bites

Purchase a good leather leash. Don't settle for nylon, chain, or fabric leashes. If your Lab pulls at all—and many do—your hands will thank me. Nylon leashes will cut into your hands, making it almost impossible to control or walk your Lab. Retractable leashes are fine for small dogs or dogs who don't pull, but not for big, strong Labs.

(© Kent and Donna Dammen)

Learn your Lab's chewing habits before allowing him to play with toys he can tear apart.

Not So Necessary Items (but Sure Nice to Have!)

I've given you the basic items in the previous section, but you're going to want to buy more than that. Most of the items I'm recommending below are very useful for pet owners.

- **Zoom-Groom comb.** These soft combs make cleaning up your Lab a breeze. The soft rubber teeth remove dead hair and mud from a Lab's coat without a lot of hassle. Most dogs who hate combs and brushes tolerate Zoom-Grooms well.
- **Pooper-scoopers.** These work better than using a shovel to pick up the ubiquitous dog poop.
- **Poop bags.** Yes, you can use supermarket bags to pick up after your Lab relieves himself while on walks, but some of those bags can have holes. I don't want to think about the consequences of that! The pre-made poop bags are often self sealing and small enough to carry to the local Dumpster.
- **Groomer's table.** You may think this is a luxury until you've thrown out your back bending over your Lab to brush and comb him. These handy tables will save you hours of chiropractor sessions. Most owners train their Labs to hop up on these tables to groom them.
- **Nail grinders.** This is an alternative to nail clippers. Some dogs scream and carry on like you were chopping off a leg instead of a tiny bit of nail when you clip their nails. A nail grinder may be less stressful for both of you.
- **Blow dryer for dogs.** Okay, I know what you're thinking—a blow dryer? Actually, they're useful in the winter to dry your Lab off quickly. Blow dryers made for dogs put out only forced air. They will not burn a dog's tender skin like human hair dryers would.
- **Toys.** These may actually be necessary if your Lab is active. Avoid latex or soft toys that can be chewed up and torn apart,

or have small pieces. Practically indestructible items made from hard rubber or nylon work best, but quite often these are the toys your dog doesn't like!

Soft stuffed toys in the shape of men or teddy bears are popular, but again, if your Lab is an aggressive chewer, you'll have bits of chew man all over the house! So watch your Lab when you give him these toys.

- **Kennel run.** If you have a fenced-in yard, this may be extraneous; however, it may save your garden and lawn. If you don't have a fenced-in yard, a kennel run is a necessity.
- **Ex-pen.** This is a wire pen that you can set up anywhere to contain your Lab. You will need one tall enough to contain an adult Lab.

ID, Please—Tags, Microchips, and Tattoos—Oh My!

It is vital for your Lab's safety and security that he have two forms of ID on him at all times. This includes tags on his regular collar as an easy means of identification. This also includes one of two more permanent methods of identification: microchips and tattoos.

Tags

Tags are a cheap form of identification. Most tags cost between $4 and $8, although if you have to have the 24-carat gold-plated tags or the tags with a blessing from St. Francis of Assisi, you're probably looking at paying between $10 and $20. They're relatively easy to obtain, too. Your vet probably has mail-in forms at his office, but you can purchase them through pet supply mail-order catalogues, online (I've actually gotten free tags from some Internet suppliers), or even from large pet supply stores. Many pet supply stores now have tag-engraving machines. For $4 to $8, you have a personalized tag that you can put on your Lab's collar right there in the store—no waiting.

Given how easy and cheap it is to put a tag on your Lab's collar, there is absolutely no reason whatsoever that he should be without tags. Make two tags—one for him to wear and one as a spare. Every day, lost dogs turn up at shelters with collars but without tags. This is inexcusable—except if the tag fell off. (It does happen.) But most owners forget or fail to put tags on their pets. Don't be one of them!

Retriever Rewards

Your Lab should always have two forms of ID on him: his tags and either a tattoo or microchip.

Lab Bites

Your Lab should never be without his collar and ID tags. All it takes is one time and he's gone without a way to have him safely returned to you.

Permanent Forms of ID—Tattoos and Microchips

But what if your Lab loses his tags or collar? Or suppose someone finds your dog and decides to keep him. Or worse yet, suppose someone *steals* your Lab? What then? The next step is to have a permanent form of ID on your Lab, either a tattoo or microchip.

You can get tattoos done at a vet clinic, or through a breed club or groomer. Both the National Dog Registry (NDR) and Tattoo-A-Pet can refer you to tattooists in your area. Vets and, sometimes, animal shelters provide microchips. Talk with your vet about both forms of permanent ID.

Tattoos are a permanent form of ID. There are two locations on a dog's body where tattoos are put: inside the ears or on the inside thigh. Inside the ears is a poor choice—dog thieves will often lop off an ear to remove the identification.

Tattooing is generally painless, but it is noisy and most dogs hate having it done. It is less expensive than microchips. You must choose a unique number for your Lab—most people choose their own social security number or their Lab's AKC registration number. However, those numbers must be registered with an ID registry.

Microchips are about the size of a grain of rice. They are encased in plastic and are activated only when a scanner is passed over them. You must have a vet perform the implantation procedure, which takes only a few seconds and causes very little discomfort. The microchip is implanted between the shoulder blades. When the scanner is passed over the chip, it reads the microchip, similar to a bar code. Then, whoever found the dog must contact the registry to look it up in the database.

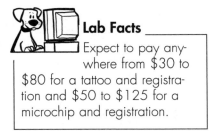

Retriever Rewards

Three ID registries for dogs are the National Dog Registry (NDR), Tattoo-A-Pet, and Home Again.

Lab Facts

Expect to pay anywhere from $30 to $80 for a tattoo and registration and $50 to $125 for a microchip and registration.

There are pluses and minuses to both identifications. First, most people don't know to check for either tattoos or microchips. If the person does find a tattoo, they probably won't know how to contact the registry. With microchips, even if the person did know to check for microchips, scanners aren't cheap and many scanners don't work with all possible microchips. There is no standard for microchips at this time, although the AKC has introduced the "Home Again" chip and registration.

Not all shelters have scanners for microchips, although Home Again and other microchip manufacturers have offered microchip scanners for free or at low cost to shelters.

But tattoo or microchip, it does no good unless its registered with a registry such as NDR, Tattoo-A-Pet, or Home Again. The person who finds your Lab needs to know how to get in touch with you and can't if your Lab isn't registered.

Bones, Chews, and Other Edible Items

There's controversy surrounding what constitutes a safe toy or chew for dogs. If you talk to pet owners—especially those on the Internet—you'll hear that so-and-so's dog died from choking on a certain toy or chew or died from an obstruction in her intestine. However, dogs love to chew—and Labs are no exception.

There probably isn't a toy or chew that's 100 percent safe. Even my own dogs—who are aggressive chewers—have torn apart what were considered indestructible items. So, talking about items such as rawhides, cow hooves, bones, and other edible chews as safe isn't appropriate. When you purchase chews or toys, keep in mind that you should buy the largest toy or chew possible—these are less likely to be swallowed whole.

Dem Bones

Most bones aren't safe for any dog. These unsafe bones include steak bones, pork chop bones, chicken and turkey bones, and other small, sharp bones. They're too easy for your Lab to chew and swallow. Some bones are sharp or can splinter. They can perforate an intestine or become lodged in your Lab's throat.

Lab Bites

There's always some danger in giving bones, rawhide, cow hooves, and other edible chews. Choose only large marrow or knuckle bones and watch your Lab's chewing habits. If he is an aggressive chewer, you may have to take the chew away to avoid a choking or obstruction hazard.

The so-called "safe" bones are large cow marrow bones and knuckle bones. I like to freeze them before giving them to my dogs—it makes them harder and less likely that pieces will break off. Still, I never leave a dog alone with a bone, and I'll take it away if they start taking pieces from them.

Some people say you should boil the bones before giving them to the dog, and others say to give them raw. I'm not sure which makes them tougher—authorities seem to argue about this, too. The plus side to boiling the bones is that it kills dangerous bacteria such as salmonella and E. coli. It's up to you. Some pet-supply stores offer entire flavored cow femurs or cooked knuckle bones. Again, that's your choice.

Regardless of what bones you give your Lab, always watch him. If he starts fracturing the bone or breaking off pieces, it's time to take the bone away.

Chew on This

Most dogs love rawhide chews. But rawhide can become dangerous if your Lab eats too much too fast. Rawhide can cause blockages in the intestine, and some dogs have choked on large pieces, so again, it's your call whether you want to take a chance on this. When you give your Lab a rawhide chew, watch to see whether he is an aggressive chewer. If he is, he may try to eat an entire rawhide bone in one sitting! Not only is that dangerous, but it may cause diarrhea due to an upset digestive tract. If you choose rawhide chews, find chews made in America. They're less likely to carry dangerous diseases than those made in countries that have experienced Mad Cow Disease.

Retriever Rewards

Cow hooves are naturally stinky. If your Lab loves them, but you hate having your house smell like a barnyard, smoked hooves are a little less smelly.

Dogs love stinky cow hooves. However, like bones, they can present an obstruction hazard. Choose the largest hooves you can so that your Lab will enjoy chewing them for hours. Remove the hoof once it is small enough to become an obstruction or choking hazard.

Other types of chews include chews that are molded from cornstarch and other plant material. There are also other chews made from dried portions of the cow or pig. As they can with hooves, bones, and rawhide, aggressive chewers can chew and swallow these quickly. It is imperative that you watch your Lab to learn his chewing habits first and take away the chew if it splinters or breaks off into parts that he can swallow whole. It may cause an obstruction or choking hazard.

Lab Bites

Unsafe toys include soft latex toys that can be chewed up or pulled apart; socks, nylons, and other pieces of clothing; anything with squeakers or whistles that can be pulled out, chewed, and swallowed; small toys or toys made for children.

Most dogs do just fine with these chews, if their owners are vigilant. However, there are enough cases of owners rushing their dogs to the emergency vet because their intestines are obstructed.

Lab Bites

Why do we have to worry about obstruction hazards? Well, dogs are able to eat items larger than they can sometimes evacuate, causing a blocked intestine. This is a very serious condition and can become life-threatening.

Puppy and Dog Food—Do's and Don'ts

Choose a high-quality, premium dog or puppy food for your Lab. At the same time, you will want to select a dog food from a recognizable manufacturer. You don't want to have to drive across town to find your Lab's food because the local pet boutique ran out of it. If your dog is under one year of age, feed him a premium puppy food; otherwise feed him a premium adult maintenance food. See Chapter 16 for more on nutrition.

If you purchase your puppy from a reputable breeder, the breeder will often include a sample of puppy food he or she is currently feeding the puppy. If it is a high-quality food, you may wish to continue feeding it to your puppy. Otherwise, you may want to switch your Lab's food over to a food you prefer. When you switch your Lab's food, do so gradually to avoid stomach upset.

Retriever Rewards

If you plan to switch your puppy or adult Lab's food, do so gradually to prevent diarrhea and stomach upset. Start with 10 percent new food and 90 percent old food the first day. The second day, feed 20 percent new food and 80 percent old food. Continue decreasing the old food by 10 percent and increasing the new food by 10 percent until you've completely switched your Lab over to the new food.

What constitutes a premium pet food? Aren't all dog foods the same? Actually, they're not. Premium pet foods usually have better-quality ingredients—they have a greater nutritional value and are highly digestible—meaning that you feed the dog less and scoop up less when cleaning up the backyard.

Pet food labels can be deceiving. Many lower-cost dog foods tout the same protein and fat percentages of premium dog foods. However, lower-cost foods often have indigestible protein or protein that is poorly metabolized. Some low-cost foods use soy or other plant proteins to increase the protein percentage in the crude analysis.

Lab Facts

By-products as ingredients in dog food are an excellent protein source for dogs. While you or I don't like the idea of chowing down on livers, hearts, and lungs, your Lab will love it. By-products provide good digestible protein and excellent nutrition—not to mention that they are often more palatable than just muscle meat.

Most veterinary nutritionists will tell you that meat is a far better protein source than soy. One look at your Lab's teeth should confirm it—dogs are carnivores. The plant material that wolves and wild dogs eat is typically predigested material in a prey animal's gut. This is why a high-quality source of meat protein is important.

Choose a dog food that has as its first ingredients a meat source. This can be chicken, meat, fish, a type of *meat meal* (chicken meal), a *by-product* (chicken by-products, for example), or a by-product meal.

Regardless of the brand of food you feed your Lab, it should say that it meets the guidelines as set forth by *AAFCO* and has been tested in feeding trials. If it does not, it cannot be considered a complete and balanced food for your pet.

Lab Lingo

AAFCO—The Association of Animal Feed Control Officials.

Meat by-products—The nonrendered, clean parts other than meat, from slaughtered mammals. This includes all organs and defatted fatty tissues. It does not include stomach or intestine contents, hair, horns, teeth, and hooves.

Meat meal—Meat with the water and fat extracted. If the label says "chicken meal," then the meal must be made from chickens.

The Least You Need to Know

- Must-have supplies for your new dog include a training crate, a bed, bowls, collars and tags, a leash, grooming supplies, and treats.
- Your Lab should have two forms of ID—tags and a permanent form of ID, such as a microchip or tattoo.
- Never leave your dog alone with a toy, bone, or chew.
- Choose a premium pet food for your Lab that meets AAFCO guidelines. If your dog is under one year old, feed him a premium puppy food. Otherwise, feed him a premium adult maintenance food.

Chapter 6

Puppy Preparedness—Bringing Your Lab Home

In This Chapter

- Dog- and puppy-proofing your home, garage, and yard
- Bringing your puppy home from the breeder
- Introducing your Lab to his new home, your family, and other pets

Before you bring your Lab home, you'll have to make sure that your home is safe for your new addition. This includes removing possible hazards from your home—including some unlikely ones you may not know you have.

In this chapter, we'll look at containment systems for your Lab, be it the old standby fence or modern innovations such as "invisible" fences. Plus, you'll see how to foil a Houdini-minded dog!

We'll also cover bringing your Lab home, his first vet trip, which should be in conjunction with his ride home from the breeder, and how to select the right veterinarian. Lastly, we'll cover introductions to both the two-footed and four-footed members of your family.

Puppy-Proofing 101

Puppies are inquisitive little critters. They love to explore. Unfortunately, puppies use their mouths like hands, and anything that a puppy puts in its mouth is fair game to chew and swallow. Even adult Labs may find some temptations too irresistible. After all, Labs are retrievers, so they are happiest with something in their mouths.

Puppies have an undiscriminating palate. They'll chew on furniture legs, electrical cords, or carpeting. Outside, many puppies pick up an affinity for landscape rock. I've known one puppy to chew on bricks and car tires.

The best way to keep a puppy from being destructive is to not give him the opportunity. Limit your Lab's exposure to mischief and he will be the perfect puppy. Leave him "home alone" and you've just told the puppy "Here's your toys—have a ball."

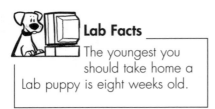

> **Lab Facts**
> The youngest you should take home a Lab puppy is eight weeks old.

The time to puppy-proof your home is now, before you bring home your new dog. The following sections give tips on securing some of the places in your home where puppies are most likely to run into trouble.

In the House

Decide where you'll allow your Lab and where is off-limits. Use baby gates or other barriers to cordon off areas that are off limits. Many experts recommend that you choose one or two rooms as "puppy areas" and expand as your Lab becomes more reliable. Many breeders recommend ex-pens—fold-up wire pens that can expand to any size space.

If you haven't done your spring cleaning, do so now—even if it's winter. You should keep out of the reach of your dog anything that is small, that can be chewed and swallowed, that is poisonous, that can fall on a dog, that is sharp, or that can break. Hide electrical cords, put away tempting items like candy and chocolate, and keep anything breakable out of reach. Some trainers recommend getting on all fours and looking at your house from a dog's-eye view. Some things that don't appear tempting from a human level are tempting to a dog.

In many respects, puppy- and dog-proofing is a lot like child-proofing one's home. Only a puppy is far more destructive than a child is. I've had puppies tear up carpet and chew it, tear down drapes, eat drywall, and gobble parts of a recliner.

Here's a partial list of items to look for when puppy-proofing your house:

- Poisonous foods, including chocolate, onions, and alcohol
- Kitchen knives
- Pesticides such as mouse and rat poisons, roach and ant baits, and insecticides
- Plates and glasses
- Shampoo, conditioner, mouthwash, and toothpaste
- Suntan lotion
- Electrical cords
- Plants
- Cleaners, including dish soap and laundry soap
- Garbage pails
- Household cleaners

Lab Bites

Chocolate is poisonous to dogs. Chocolate contains a substance called theobromine, which can kill a dog if ingested in large quantities. Dark, bittersweet, or baker's chocolate is more poisonous than milk chocolate. Make sure your children understand in no uncertain terms that they are not to feed chocolate to the dog.

Lab Bites

Did you know that the fluoride in human toothpaste is poisonous to dogs? Never use human toothpaste on dogs. Keep your toothpaste in the medicine cabinet away from your inquisitive Lab.

- Candles, scented oils, and scented air fresheners
- Medications, including ibuprofen (Advil, Motrin), acetaminophen (Tylenol), and aspirin
- Vitamins
- Dental floss
- Children's toys
- Pennies and other coins
- Socks and other clothing items
- Sewing needles, craft kits, and so on
- Glass knickknacks
- Pens, paper, and other small items that may be chewed or swallowed
- Paper shredder
- Wood stove, kitchen stove, and furnaces
- Batteries
- String, rubber bands, and paper clips
- Drapery cords—may hang a puppy

Retriever Rewards

Tape the phone numbers for your veterinarian, local poison control center, and a 24-hour emergency vet to your phone. That way, if there is an emergency, you'll have the numbers handy.

In the Garage

The garage is a particularly hazardous place for your Lab. You should not allow your Lab in the garage because of all the potential poisons and dangerous substances there. Radiators leak, causing the potential for antifreeze poisoning. Another poison in the garage is windshield-washing fluid, which is just as dangerous as antifreeze.

Retriever Rewards

Antifreeze manufacturers have developed safer antifreeze for people with pets and small children. The antifreeze is still toxic, but only in larger quantities—a dog is unlikely to become seriously sick if he drinks from a puddle with a small amount of "safer" antifreeze mixed in.

While motor oil and transmission fluids aren't deadly if consumed alone, they can be if they are mixed with antifreeze. They certainly aren't healthy for your Lab, and will cause severe gastric upsets. Other poisonous items a dog might encounter in the garage include rat and mouse poisons, insecticides, herbicides, and fertilizers.

Hardware poses a hazard as well. Nails, screws, washers, and nuts can be swallowed. Sharp items such as saws can cut your Lab. Trash cans are always a temptation.

Lab Bites

Most people know that antifreeze is poisonous to pets, but did you know that windshield-wiper fluid is just as poisonous? Keep both the windshield-wiper fluid and antifreeze away from your Lab.

Backyard Blues

If you haven't put up a fence or some kind of containment system for your Lab, do so now. Your Lab deserves to be safe and happy. Allowing your dog to run loose is irresponsible, at best. At worst, he'll be a nuisance and a danger to both himself and others.

In the city and suburbs, the chance for your dog to be hit by a car is very good. There aren't too many car-wise dogs out there, and you'll find even the most street-wise mutts dead in a ditch. Loose dogs run in packs, getting into neighbors' garbage, becoming aggressive toward people and children, attacking and killing other people's pets, and being a general danger. Most communities have laws against letting a dog run loose. You can be fined if you let your Lab run loose.

(© Jacky Sachs)

Although Labs love to run, never allow yours to run loose. Keep him behind a fence or other containment system when you're not at home.

In the country, dogs routinely harass and kill livestock and valuable game animals. In many rural areas, it is legal for farmers, ranchers, and game wardens to shoot stray dogs. Dogs routinely tangle with skunks, porcupines, and raccoons. A loose dog has a greater chance of contracting rabies. And many stray dogs provide a food source for coyotes and mountain lions.

It's not kind to let a dog run loose. Your Lab will be happier and healthier safe at home, enjoying your company. If you feel you don't have time to exercise your Lab, perhaps you should reconsider your choice to own a dog.

The best containment system is a six-foot fence or a kennel run. Shorter fences will work for puppies, but adolescent dogs with Houdini-like antics can jump over four-foot fences.

"Invisible fences" and pet containment systems will work *provided* that the owner properly trains the dog. These systems will *not* work without proper training. Don't turn your puppy loose in your yard and expect it to work. The downside to electronic pet-containment systems is that these systems do nothing to keep out other dogs. Your Lab may be at the mercy of loose dogs and other potential threats. If you have an unspayed female, the invisible fence will not deter unwanted suitors.

Lab Bites

The pods from the Black Locust tree are deadly if ingested. These pods are indistinguishable from the Honey Locust tree (which is harmless). If you have one in your yard, be certain that the pods won't fall in an area where your Lab will be.

Lab Facts

A Houdini dog is made, not born, although some breeds are naturally more inclined to become escape artists than others. Most Labs are content to be homebodies, but that's a small consolation if your Lab proves otherwise

People create Houdini dogs in two ways:

- By putting up inferior barriers
- By not giving their dogs enough to do

Houdini dogs are typically very smart dogs who are bored. Their owners put up an inferior barrier and the Houdini dog figures a way around it. The owner ups the barrier slightly, and the dog figures another way around. It then becomes a game of one-upmanship.

Foil the Houdini dog by putting up good fences and giving him plenty of activities.

Once you've solved your containment system, the next step is to look for potential hazards in the yard. Contact your local poison-control center or state agricultural office for a listing of possible poisonous plants in your area. Many ornamental plants and trees are poisonous. Although some mushrooms are benign, it's best to treat all mushrooms as poisonous and remove them.

(© Katherine Shaver)

Your Lab will be happy inside his own fence. This is Shalane Lady Hannah inside her fence.

But plants aren't the only hazard in your yard. Many puppies and some dogs enjoy ingesting landscaping rock, which can cause a serious obstruction. Chemicals and fertilizers put on your lawn can be absorbed through the skin or licked off paw pads. Sharp edging can cut paws. If you have a pool or hot tub, be certain to cordon it off. While Labs are great swimmers, dogs have drowned in pools by not knowing how to climb out. Likewise, high decks can present a falling hazard.

Bringing Puppy Home

Bring your Lab home when you have enough time to spend with him. Take time off from work or school to be with your new pet. If you can't take time off, try picking up your Lab from the breeder on a Friday so that you will have the weekend to spend with him.

> **Retriever Rewards**
>
> Bring your Labrador home in a crate. Don't use a box, and don't allow him to run loose in the car.

Don't bring a new addition home around Christmas or the holidays. Quite often, the holidays are too hectic to spend enough time with your puppy.

When you go to the breeder to pick up your Lab, bring the crate that we told you to purchase in Chapter 5. Even if you're bringing someone along, bring a travel crate to carry your new pet home. A loose puppy is dangerous in the car. The puppy can slip from the passenger's arms and climb underfoot or, worse, jump from the window.

The Breeder's Take-Home Package

The breeder should have all your paperwork together. This should include your Lab's AKC papers, copies of the parents' certifications and AKC records, the breeder's contract, your Lab's pedigree, and your Lab's health records. The breeder may include a puppy care package with samples of puppy food and a toy. Never accept a breeder's promise that "the papers will be along later." You have no recourse with the AKC if they are not!

First Stop: The Veterinarian

Your first stop should be at the veterinarian, to be certain that your Lab is in good health. Make an appointment with the veterinarian ahead of time so that you can bring your puppy to the clinic right from the breeder's home.

The veterinarian may want a stool sample, so bring a plastic baggie along in case the opportunity to collect one arises. Give the vet your Lab's health record. The veterinarian should examine your Lab for any problems and vaccinate him if needed at this time. Follow your veterinarian's recommendations regarding vaccinations and other health issues.

Don't Have a Puppy Surprise Party

Bringing your new pet home can be exciting for everyone, but also a little scary for the dog. Don't have a puppy surprise party. Instead, plan to keep the excitement to a minimum. When you come home, give your Lab a chance to relieve himself. He may forget in the excitement to relieve himself, so walk him on a leash until he calms down. Then, bring him inside.

Don't have everyone crowd around him all at once. That can be very scary. Instead, let your Lab explore his new environment. Then, have your family members greet your new pet—one at a time. Give your Lab a chance to settle down.

> **Retriever Rewards**
>
> Put your Lab's crate in your bedroom when you both go to sleep. If your Lab cries, your presence will reassure him. You can also rap on the crate and tell him, "No! Quiet!" without leaving your bed.

Don't introduce other family pets just yet. This environment is very new and your Lab needs time to adjust to it.

Naturally, your Lab will be sniffing all over. But if he sniffs and circles, or looks like he may squat, take him outside on a leash. If he has an "accident," usher him out quickly and clean the area with soap and water, followed by white vinegar and water or enzymatic cleaner.

It will take some time for your Lab to become used to you and your family. Use the next several days to teach your Lab your routine.

Introductions to Other Family Pets

Don't introduce the other family pets when you first bring home your new Lab. Instead, give your new pet a chance to adjust to his new surroundings.

If your other pet is a dog, the best thing to do is introduce them in a neutral place. Usually a park works well. You and another family member or friend should take the pets to the park on leash.

Walk up to each other and let them sniff and greet each other. If there is any sign of aggression, *correct* it immediately. Otherwise, if your dogs are being friendly, allow them to play, but continue to be watchful for any sign of aggression.

If your dogs show any aggression, you may have to keep them separate for a while. This means keeping them crated when you can't watch them. Have supervised play sessions and correct any aggressive behavior by saying "No!" and putting the dogs in a sit or down stay. If your other dog is aggressive toward your Lab, you may have to consult an animal behaviorist.

If your Lab is a young puppy, you may introduce him to the cat by letting the cat wander in and meet the puppy on his own terms. If your Lab is an adult, you may want to keep the cat in another part of the house so that your Lab can get used to the cat's scent. Then, introduce your Lab to the cat by keeping the Lab on leash. Correct any aggressive behavior and offer your Lab treats to focus his attention away from the cat. Reward good behavior.

Lab Lingo

Correct—Doing something that causes undesirable behavior to cease.

The Least You Need to Know

- Puppy-proofing your home requires that you remove all tempting items from the puppy's reach, including electrical cords, medications, clothing, breakable items, and small items that can be chewed and swallowed.
- Don't keep your Lab in the garage. There are too many poisonous and dangerous things there.
- Your Lab needs a fenced-in yard or a kennel run. Don't allow your Lab to run loose!
- Carry your Lab home from the breeder in a crate and stop off at the vet on the way home for vaccinations and a check-up.
- Don't crowd your Lab when you arrive home. Let him relieve himself and explore his new surroundings.

Chapter 7

Crates and Housetraining

In This Chapter

- What's a crate, and isn't it cruel?
- How to crate train a puppy and an older dog
- Housetraining do's and don'ts
- Cleaning up "accidents"

The crate is perhaps one of the greatest tools a pet owner can have. Unfortunately, it's also the most misunderstood. In this chapter, you'll learn why crates aren't cruel and why most dogs love theirs. You'll also learn why you should use one in housebreaking and training.

But crate training isn't just a matter of popping your Lab into a crate. You need to train your Lab to use it properly. Both puppies and older dogs can benefit from crate training when you do it right.

In this chapter, we also cover housetraining; that is, *housebreaking* in older terms. Housetraining is easy when you know the tricks. What's more, you don't have to punish your Lab puppy for having an accident.

All About Crates

What's a crate? To the nondog person, the crate may look like a cage or a shipping container. To the professional dog trainer, the crate is a way of containing a dog and keeping him safe and out of mischief. To the dog, the crate feels like a comfortable den.

Trainers use crates to housetrain dogs and to teach dogs good manners. Dogs and puppies who are crate trained become model pets because they don't learn bad habits such as destructive behavior and chewing inappropriate items.

Crates come in a variety of materials and sizes. When you choose a crate, choose one with a good locking mechanism—preferably with two latches. You can choose either wire or plastic. If you choose wire, choose one with a heavy enough gauge that your Lab won't chew through it. If you purchase a plastic travel crate, be sure it meets the FAA requirements for airline travel, in case you ever fly with your Lab. There are some very lightweight crates made from fabric and PVC pipe. Do not purchase these; they are intended only for obedience-trained dogs and only for a very brief time.

Lab Facts

Crates simulate an animal's den in the wild. All dogs have a denning instinct. Your Lab will be happier if he has a "den" all his own.

Lab Bites

Don't use your Lab's crate as punishment. Instead, use it as a safe place to put him and a place to reward him. Otherwise, he will look at it negatively.

The crate should be large enough for an adult Lab to stand up, turn around, and lie down in comfortably. If you wish, you can purchase a smaller puppy crate (usually fairly inexpensive) to start and then purchase an adult crate as your Lab gets older.

If you purchase an adult crate for a puppy, be certain to cordon off a portion of the crate to fit the puppy. Otherwise, the puppy will have enough room to relieve himself in the crate and will thwart your housebreaking efforts.

Your Lab's crate will be his spot when you can't watch him. It'll be a safe place for him when workmen come in and out of your house and accidentally leave the doors open. It'll be a place where your Lab stays when he trembles at thunder or the Fourth of July fireworks.

Why Crate Training Is *Not* Cruel

When uninformed people see dogs in crates, the first thing they think is "How cruel!" This is strictly an anthropomorphism of their own feelings. The dog in the crate is probably thinking "I'm in a strange, scary place—glad I'm in my crate!" The crate is a safe place—it's reassuring, like a child's blanket.

Wolves, coyotes, foxes, and other wild dogs generally don't sleep outdoors (except maybe to nap in the sun). The wild is a dangerous place, and being caught in the open could mean death. This is why wolves and other wild dogs sleep in dens.

Dens aren't very roomy. They're usually tight quarters to trap the wolf's body heat in cold weather. The wolf will seek shelter in inclement weather or danger. This natural denning instinct is in all dogs—even your Lab!

Think of the wolf's den when you see the crate. Most dogs are content to lie in it without much of a fuss. In many cases, it's safer than leaving your Lab to roam the house, looking for items to chew.

I've had dogs lie in their crates snoozing away while the crate doors were open. I've had dogs "hide" in their crates during severe thunderstorms. If my dogs truly hated their crates, they wouldn't rush into them so readily.

Lab Facts

Most dogs enjoy their crates. In my house, you'll often catch one snoozing in a crate with the door open.

Most dogs do extremely well with crate training. A few older dogs who have not been crate trained may have some difficulties adjusting. Usually with proper training, this isn't an issue.

Alternatives to Crates

Unfortunately, there aren't too many alternatives to crates. There's a reason why so many trainers use them: They work.

One alternative is the ex-pen, or exercise pen. The ex-pen is like a large, open-air crate. Unfortunately, many dogs can jump, climb, or knock down an ex-pen. A big Lab has no problems scaling one of these. Another problem with ex-pens is that they may not be small enough to aid in housetraining. Your Lab may learn to soil a small corner of the ex-pen, thus foiling any attempts to housetrain him. Dogs don't like soiling their own beds and won't urinate or defecate until let out. If the crate or ex-pen is too big, the dog has room to soil the area.

Another alternative is confining your Lab to a small room in the house. However, this does not prevent your Lab from chewing up anything inside the room. Unless the room is tiny, you may have the same problems housetraining your Lab in a small room as you would in an ex-pen.

(© Katherine Shaver)

Puppies can get in an extraordinary amount of trouble if not kept contained.

Crate Training 101

So, how do you begin crate training? First, select the place where you'll put the crate—preferably in a spot not far from activity in the house. Your puppy's crate will need to be in your bedroom at night, so you might want to have two crates to avoid this.

Feed your Lab his meals in his crate. Toss his treats into the crate so that he must go in to eat them. Give him his chews in the crate. Have him associate the crate with good things.

Retriever Rewards

Some trainers recommend giving your puppy a hot-water bottle filled with warm water wrapped in a towel inside the crate and leaving an old-fashioned ticking alarm clock (with the alarm turned off) on top of the crate. The ticking simulates the beating of mom's heart and the hot-water bottle is comforting like littermates.

While he's eating, close the door for a while. Then, open it again and let him out when you can watch him. When you want him to go into his crate, toss a treat in and then close the door when he goes inside.

Some puppies will fuss. But if you give your dog a nice marrow bone, it may not even occur to him that the crate door is closed.

Bedtime Is Also Crate Time

At bedtime, bring your puppy's crate to the bedroom and put him in it for the night. He may cry—especially if this is his first night away from home. You can try the old "hot water bottle and clock trick," or you can just rap on his crate and tell him to be quiet.

It's very important to have your Lab sleep in your bedroom. It will help him bond to you. However, it is not a good idea to let your Lab sleep in bed with you. You will look too much like a littermate.

If he has dominant tendencies, you may have dominance problems later. That's why the crate comes in handy at bedtime, too.

Lab Bites

Have your Lab sleep in your bedroom—but not in your bed! If your Lab sleeps in your bed, you have made him into an equal and he may later challenge you for dominance.

Crate Training for Older Dogs

Crate train an older Lab as you would a puppy. Feed him his meals in his crate, toss treats into his crate to get him to go in, and give him chews in his crate.

Occasionally, you'll find an adult dog resistant to crate training, but this is rare. If your adult Lab has trouble adjusting to his crate, consider a crate alternative or seek the help of a professional trainer.

Housetraining 101

Housetraining is the first big challenge for the Lab owner. The good news is that puppies and dogs don't want to soil their beds unless they absolutely have to. You can take advantage of this instinct by containing your Lab in a small area such as a crate.

Whenever you release your Lab from the crate, the first trip should be outside so that your Lab can relieve himself. Otherwise, the first thing your Lab will do is relieve himself on your floor. The choice is yours. Pick up your Lab puppy or snap a leash on his collar (if he is too big to carry) and bring him outside to an appropriate place. Don't just praise him when he goes—let him know that he is the most wonderful Labrador in the entire universe! Give him a treat, if you'd like.

Retriever Rewards

Carry poop bags whenever you walk your Lab. Nobody likes "stepping in it," and in many cities, you're required to pick up after your dog or face large fines.

That's the basics to housetraining or housebreaking. Show your Lab the appropriate spot to "go" and then praise him when he does that. But what about keeping him from going inside? Like all good training, you enforce the correct behavior and prevent the incorrect behavior.

A Housetraining Schedule

Labs do well on schedules. If you do something more than once at a certain time (let's say, feed him), you're guaranteed that by the third day, your Lab will be demanding dinner on schedule (or a little before). You can use a schedule to housebreak your Lab. The following schedule works well to walk or put your Lab outside for a "potty break":

- First thing in the morning
- After breakfast
- Before you go to work or school
- At noontime (if the puppy is under three months)
- After lunch (if the puppy is under three months)
- When you return home from work or school
- After dinner
- After playtime
- Before bedtime

You may feel more like a doggie doorman than a pet owner with a schedule like this. However, it doesn't take long for a conscientious Lab owner and the Lab to adjust to this schedule. As your Lab grows older, you can eliminate some of the outdoor trips.

Potty on Command

If you must walk your Lab because you live in the city or don't have a fenced-in yard, this schedule may seem daunting. However, there's good news: You can train your Lab to "go potty" on command! Every time your Lab "goes," you need to give him a command such as "potty," "hurry up," or whatever you'd like. Be careful what you choose—one of my own dogs knew the words "go potty," and there was nothing more embarrassing than saying that out in public!

Lab Bites

Don't paper train! Ever. Paper training confuses your Lab by making him think that he must "potty" in the house. You'll have a tougher time breaking him of paper training when you want him to go outside.

Housetraining "Don'ts"

- **Don't paper train.** This will just confuse your Lab into thinking it's okay to "potty" in the house.
- **Don't rub his nose in it.** What are you trying to teach your Lab? You're trying to teach him not to "go" in the house—not that you're a mean person!
- **Don't scream or yell.** You can't train a dog who's terrified of you.
- **Don't correct him if it's diarrhea.** Your Lab really couldn't help it.
- **Don't make your Lab "hold it" for more than nine hours** (or four or five hours for a pup younger than six months). This is really unfair to him.

Retriever Rewards

Most puppies need to be let out after they sleep, eat, drink, or play. Anticipate the need and you'll have fewer accidents.

Housetraining "Do's"

- **Put your Lab on a schedule.** This will make it easier for him to hold it.
- **Let your Lab out after feeding and playing.**

- **Put your Lab in a crate when you can't watch him.** This will prevent him from "going" in the house behind your back until he's housebroken.
- **If your Lab starts circling or squats, whisk him outside.** Praise him when he goes outside.
- **Teach your Lab to "potty" on command.**

Uh-oh! What to Do with Accidents

You've caught your Lab "in the act." What do you do?

First, you can say "No! No!" to surprise him and interrupt what he's doing. Then you whisk him outside as quickly as possible. Once he starts urinating and defecating there, praise him!

What if you find a "present" for you on the floor? Trainers are somewhat in disagreement here. Some say you shouldn't punish him, whereas others say that you should. Some say you can punish, but only if the poop is warm. Well, I don't believe in checking the poop so thoroughly, so I'll give you my own compromise. The straight poop, if you would.

Retriever Rewards

Use white vinegar and water or pet enzymatic cleaner to clean up "accidents." These products will help neutralize the odor that will encourage your Lab to use that spot again. Don't use ammonia-based cleaning products because urine has ammonia in it.

I show my dogs the mess and tell them how bad they are. I don't yell or scream; I don't drag them over to it; I don't stick their noses in it; I just show it to them. Then, I pick up the mess, put it outside, and then put them outside to do their business. This seems to work with both adults and puppies.

Use an enzymatic cleaner to clean up the mess and remove the odor. Don't use household cleaning supplies—many contain ammonia, which will emphasize any urine smells. I recommend Nature's Miracle, but there are also some very effective brands by other manufacturers.

If you're out of enzymatic cleaner—and this usually occurs at 11 P.M., when the pet-supply stores are closed—you can clean the mess up with soap and water and follow it up with white vinegar and water.

The Least You Need to Know

- Crates are useful training items that help with housebreaking and preventing destructive behavior. They are not cruel.
- Crate-train your dog by feeding him his meals in it, tossing treats into it, and generally making him associate it with good things.
- You can housebreak your Lab by putting him on a schedule.
- Don't rub your puppy's nose in his poop. Instead, show him the mess, tell him "bad dog," and put both him and the mess outside.
- Clean up messes using a special ezymatic cleaner formulated for cleaning up after dogs; or, in a pinch, you can use soap and water followed by white vinegar and water.

Part 3

Dog Training 101

Dog training has come a long way since the old snap-the-leash methodologies. Nowadays, trainers use a variety of positive-reinforcement techniques to train dogs in a fun and positive manner.

Training your Lab requires knowledge in dog behavior. To understand dog behavior, you must understand wolf behavior. Dogs, like wolves, are pack animals. Dogs understand hierarchy and respect it. In Part 3, I'll show you the basics of how to be "top dog" to your Lab.

In Part 3, I also discuss the disadvantages to "going it alone" and give you tips for selecting the right dog trainer. I show you how to teach your Lab the basic commands and give you the "secrets" that every dog trainer knows. And there's a whole chapter on what to do when a good dog does bad things.

Chapter 8

Alpha, Beta, Gamma: Greek Alphabet Soup and How It Relates to Your Lab's Behavior

In This Chapter

- What behavior has your Lab inherited from wolves?
- What is an alpha dog and how can you be one?
- How to communicate with your Lab
- How to recognize and curb aggressive alpha behavior

People, as a rule, speak poor dog. In the past few hundred years, humans have moved from an agricultural society to an industrial society where we have little contact with other species. In the transition, more and more people have lost their dog-bilingual abilities.

Dogs, though, are still dogs and have inherited their communication and behavior from wolves. You can, however, learn to speak dog and communicate more effectively with your Lab.

Lab Lingo

Alpha dog—A dog who has a dominant personality.

Alpha—When trainers talk about "alpha," they are talking about who is in charge.

In this chapter, we cover the basic pack structure and dog pack behavior. We go over what *alpha* means and what you have to do to become alpha in your Lab's eyes. We'll also cover the warning signs of a dominant dog and how you can prevent aggression and other troublesome problems.

How Wolves Act

All dogs are descendants of wolves. Although there are marked differences between man's best friend and his wild ancestor, much of the dog's behavior is inherited from wolves.

Wolves exhibit pack behavior. Two wolves are in charge of the pack—a male and female, called the alpha pair. Often—although not always—they are the main breeding pair. The whole pack works toward ensuring the survival of the pups of the alpha pair.

Lab Facts

Dogs are naturally pack animals. Because dogs think of humans as just part of the pack, they have been able to bond to humans and become "man's best friend."

Packs enable wolves to hunt and bring down large game. It is much harder for a single wolf to bring down an elk or moose than it is for a pack to do it. Hunting such large game puts the individual at greater risk than in a pack, where there are numerous players. The alpha wolves often have a crucial role in the hunt, so they get to eat first, thus ensuring their survival and the survival of the pack.

There is a pack hierarchy below the alpha wolves—each wolf has its place, whether in the middle or at the bottom. This may seem grossly unfair to us humans, but this hierarchy has worked for wolves for thousands of years.

How Dogs Act

You may be surprised to learn that all dogs have this basic pack instinct to some degree. This pack behavior has enabled humans to make dogs into working companions and eventually pets. Dogs bond to humans as part of their "pack." Because dogs maintain a need for hierarchy, however, there are various degrees to the "alpha" or dominant personality that your dog might have.

At one extreme is the alpha dog. This dog is normally a very challenging personality. He or she will exhibit dominant traits such as leg-lifting and marking, challenging your authority, and other unpleasant behavior. The alpha is also very confident as well. He or she will be more bold than other dogs.

At the other extreme is an *omega* personality. This dog is very submissive and tentative. He will not challenge you, and instead may cringe in fear. This dog can become a fear-biter if you do not train and socialize him properly.

Lab Lingo

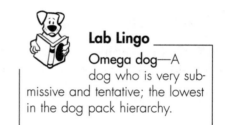

Omega dog—A dog who is very submissive and tentative; the lowest in the dog pack hierarchy.

Most dogs are somewhere in between. Many Labs will have some assertiveness that you can channel into energy for working, show, or other activities. However, if you allow this dominance behavior to continue unchecked, you may end up with an unruly or even aggressive dog.

How to Be the Alpha to Your Dog

Becoming an alpha to your Lab doesn't mean bullying him! On the contrary—you want to earn your Lab's respect. You work better for people whom you respect and admire, and your Lab is no different. He will want to please you that much more if he respects you.

R-E-S-P-E-C-T

How do you earn your Lab's respect? By being fair and consistent. Dogs require consistency in their lives. Always be consistent in your praise and correction. Don't correct your Lab for one action and then allow it at another time. Never punish your Lab for something he doesn't understand or can't do. Don't get angry, yell, or scream. This behavior will confuse him.

Often when your Lab does something wrong, it is because he doesn't understand or has misinterpreted what you want him to do. Punishing your Lab for something he doesn't understand is terribly unfair. Instead, you need to show him what the correct behavior is and praise him when he does it.

Enforce Your Alpha Role

Being alpha means enforcing your alpha role. This means that you should act as though you are in charge. You should relate to your Lab as if he's a companion, but one who is a subordinate and not an equal. Here are some ways you can do that:

- **Don't put yourself in compromising positions**. Games such as tug-of-war and wrestling make you look like an equal or a subordinate to your Lab.

> **Lab Bites**
>
> Don't play tug-of-war and other games that put you on the same level as your Lab. Don't roughhouse or wrestle with him. It puts you in a compromising position.

- **Don't let your Lab sleep in the bed with you.** It makes you look like a littermate.
- **Feed your Lab after you eat dinner**. Alphas always eat first.
- **Have your Lab sit and wait while you fix his dinner**. Dinnertime can often be chaotic. Insist on good manners.
- **Don't free feed.** Free feeding means to leave the food out all the time so that your dog can eat it whenever he chooses. This

practice gives your Lab control of his dinnertime instead of looking to you for his meals.

Retriever Rewards

Feed your Lab separate meals instead of free feeding. It will make him look to you for his meals instead of having them magically appear in his bowl.

- **Don't give treats just because your Lab exists.** Instead, have your Lab perform a command or trick, such as sitting, speaking, or shaking hands.
- **Never give a command you aren't willing or able to enforce.** You will have shown your Lab that he can disobey you if he feels like it.
- **Don't allow your Lab to climb up on furniture uninvited.**
- **Don't allow your Lab to "mount" you.** This is a dominance maneuver.
- **Practice training commands for 5 to 10 minutes every day.**
- **Practice sit-stays and down-stays.** This will enforce good behavior. (See Chapter 10 for more about these commands.)
- **Exercise with your Lab.** An active Lab is a happy Lab and one less likely to have behavioral problems.

How to Speak Dog

Part of becoming alpha is knowing what your dog is saying to you and how to react to him. Dogs use a variety of vocal, facial, and body expressions to communicate. Most people think that a dog wagging her tail means that she's happy. Well, sometimes …

Lab Bites

A dog with a wagging tail doesn't necessarily mean he is happy or friendly. Look at the entire dog's expression—not just the tail. Dogs can wag their tails in aggressive or fearful behavior as well!

Tail-wagging can occur with aggressive or insecure behavior as well as happy behavior. What's important is the combination of expressions. A tail wagging stiffly with head raised and hackles up means aggression, whereas a lowered body and cheerful wag of the tail may mean play or happiness. Expressions depend on the breed and dog; some dogs for example, may show varying degrees of behaviors.

Here are some general expressions and their meanings:

- **Submissive or insecure:** The dog's head is lowered, ears are back, body is cringing, and his tail may wag. The dog avoids eye contact. Many people mistake this behavior for a "guilty" look or fearfulness.
- **Happy:** The dog's head is at level height, his tail and body wag, and he may circle with little jumps. Ears may be back or forward, depending on the level of excitement.
- **Fearful:** Submissive behavior that may be combined with either barking in short yips or growling. The dog is trying to back away from whatever it is that's causing fear. His tail is tucked.
- **Challenge:** The dog stands tall and stiff. He may walk stiff-legged. His tail may wag slowly and be upright as a flag in a breeze. The dog maintains eye contact. His *hackles* may or may not be up. He might be fearful as well—and is trying to bluff.

Lab Lingo

Hackles—The hair along the shoulders and back of the neck. These will stand straight out when the dog is excited, fearful, or angry.

- **Aggression:** Growling or snarling. Maintains eye contact. Keeps a challenge position or may lower his head slightly.

Watch your Lab for these various expressions. Note that these are generalizations and some dogs may show some, all, or none of these behaviors.

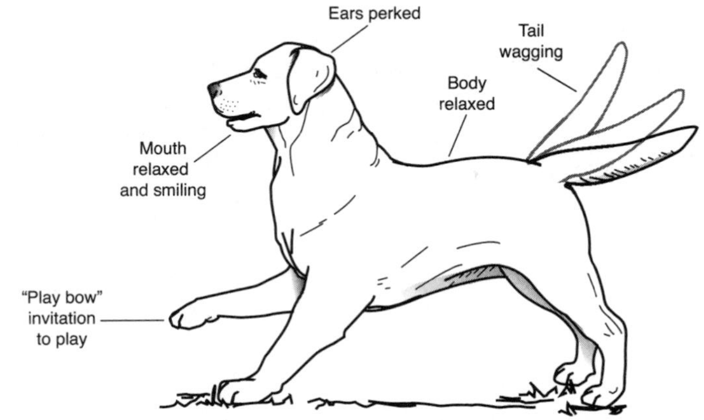

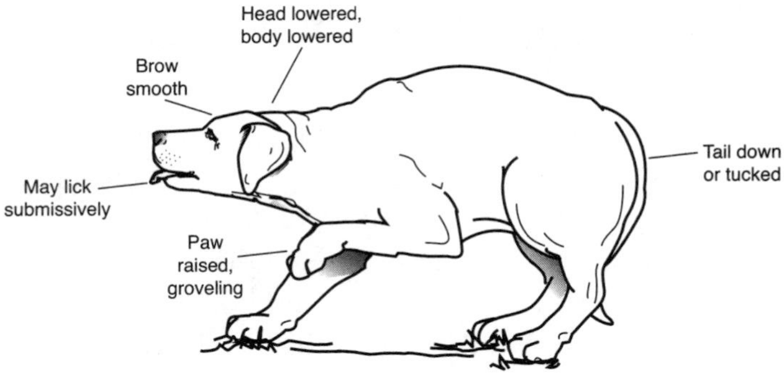

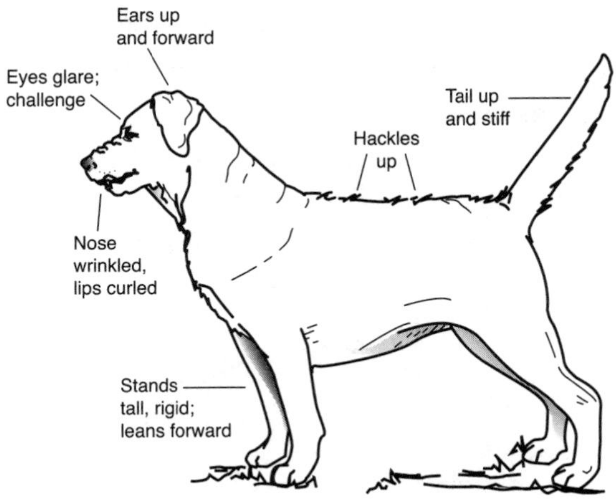

Your Lab's many expressions. From the top: happy or playful; fearful or very submissive; aggressive—note that the tail may wag stiffly.

Lab Bites

Some books in the past have recommended "alpha rolls" and "alpha shakes" to force compliance. Never use these techniques except under the guidance of a professional behaviorist and in extreme dominance aggression. Your dog may bite you out of fear. These techniques should be used only under extreme circumstances in dealing with aggression, and even then the dog should be muzzled. Never use these techniques for everyday training.

Recognizing Signs of Dominance Aggression—Stopping Trouble Before It Starts

There are various types of aggression, but the one that seems to cause the most problems is dominance behavior. The behavior starts innocently enough—your Lab mouths you, he grumbles when you push him off the couch, or he ignores a command he knows well. Surprisingly, this may be the start of something much more sinister if you don't stop it now. Don't let it escalate to the point where the behavior gets out of control.

If your Lab starts acting snotty—ignoring your commands, growling, lifting his leg indoors—it's time for a trip to the vet. Some biological conditions manifest themselves as behavior problems. Note that very young puppies (that is, puppies less than four months) should not show any signs of aggression toward you. If yours does, have him examined by a vet right away.

Lab Facts

Pain can cause aggressive signs. Teething puppies often have sore mouths and act aggressively if you handle their mouths. Hip dysplasia can be very painful, so touching the dog's hindquarters could elicit aggressive behavior.

If your Lab doesn't have any underlying health problems, the next step is to start enforcing your alpha position now. (See "Enforce Your Alpha Role," earlier in this chapter). This includes training and enforcing your status as alpha. If the problem is growling while on the couch, make the furniture and bed off-limits. Stop free-feeding your Lab if you're doing it. Start training him daily.

If you aren't planning to show your Lab in conformation shows, spay or neuter him as early as practical. (Most vets recommend doing it at six months, but some spay or neuter as early as eight weeks.) Neutering has proven to help curb many behavior problems in males. In my own experience, spaying reduces aggression and dominance behavior in females as well.

One trick in the trainer's repertoire is a little bonding technique I learned early on. If your Lab is being destructive or is marking while you aren't looking, get a long leash (10 feet or so) and hook one end to his collar. Tie the end to your belt or belt loop while your Lab is in the house. Now, he has to go where you go and has to focus on you. When you can't watch your Lab, you put him in his crate. Simple.

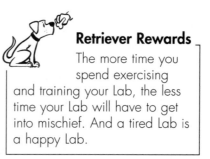

Retriever Rewards

The more time you spend exercising and training your Lab, the less time your Lab will have to get into mischief. And a tired Lab is a happy Lab.

This technique works wonders for many dogs if the owner is consistent and continues with it for a month or more. However, by the time many owners seek help, the dog is well beyond a simple fix. The trick is to not allow the problem to progress this far.

If you have a serious problem—that is, real aggression, such as biting and threatening growls that make you afraid—consult a professional behaviorist immediately.

The Least You Need to Know

- Dogs have inherited pack behavior from wolves.
- Your Lab expects for you to be alpha, that is, a benevolent leader and someone to respect. Do so by being fair and consistent and enforcing all rules.
- Learn to read your Lab's body language so that you will have a better communication with him as his alpha. It's complex, but with a little observation, you'll be able to speak good "dog."
- Recognize the beginning signs of dominance aggression. Most start innocently enough, but by the time there is real trouble, you may need to seek a professional trainer.

Chapter 9

Professional Training Lab

In This Chapter

- Can you train your Lab by yourself or do you need a professional trainer?
- How to find the right trainer for you and your Lab
- Obedience training and other classes
- An introduction to dog sports training

Your Lab will need obedience training, but should you train him yourself? Although dog training isn't brain surgery, training your dog from a book is a little like teaching a doctor through correspondence courses. I suppose you could do it, but there's no guarantee on the results.

The good news is that there are many reputable trainers out there who know the latest and most effective training methods. In this chapter, we'll look at finding a trainer and what training classes are available. You'll also get a first look at other, more advanced, training classes that prepare your dog for competition.

Should You Train Your Lab by Yourself?

A well-trained Lab is a joy to own. You can take him almost anywhere and do almost anything with him. He's well behaved in the car, in the park, on a boat, in the forest, or in a crowd. Unfortunately, these dogs are in the minority.

When you see an ill-behaved dog, it's not the dog's fault. It's the owner's fault for failing to train the dog properly. Many dog owners have good intentions. They may make an honest effort to train their dogs. Realistically, though, they don't have the time or the patience to wade through training manuals to learn the right techniques.

> **Retriever Rewards**
>
> If you are short on time, patience, and experience, you're better off finding a professional dog trainer than trying to do it on your own.

If you admit that you're one of these people—with good intentions but not enough time, patience, or experience—kudos to you! Seek a professional trainer to help you train your Lab. It'll still take time, but you'll learn shortcuts you may never learn on your own.

(© Kent and Donna Dannen)

A Lab in obedience training. A good trainer will teach you how to train your Lab.

A good professional trainer trains *you* to train your Lab. This is important. You don't want to pay a lot of money and hand your dog off to someone to train, only to have your dog look to the trainer to obey—not you. Training classes not only teach you how to train, but they also strengthen the bond between both you and your Lab.

If you do decide to "go it alone," that's okay, too. If at any time you don't think you're succeeding, you can still sign up for basic obedience class. You *can* teach an old dog new tricks and it's never too late to learn.

Lab Facts

A good dog trainer will teach *you* how to train your Lab. The best trainers focus on the bond between you and your Lab.

Lab Lingo

Positive reinforcement—A training technique that rewards the dog for behaving in the correct manner. It is a form of operant conditioning that uses little, if any, coercion or punishment. Both owners and dogs enjoy this training.

Operant conditioning—A method of learning in which the animal learns according to its actions; in other words, he does something and gets a reward or punishment as a result of his actions and modifies his behavior accordingly.

Looking for the Right Trainer

How do you find a reputable dog trainer? Talk to your dog-owning friends, your Lab's breeder, and your veterinarian. Many will have recommendations for trainers in your area. You can also find trainers by talking to people whose dogs compete in conformation, obedience, and agility shows (see "Take Your Training Further: Professional Dog Sports," later in this chapter). Most have recommendations.

If you're unable to get recommendations, you may want to check the yellow pages under "Dog Trainers." Some community colleges and pet-supply stores also offer obedience classes, but be careful! Bargain trainers are often no bargain.

When choosing a trainer, ask whether you can drop in and watch the trainer run a class. The trainer should be happy to let you watch him work. If he doesn't want you to watch because you might "steal his secrets," consider another trainer.

The trainer should be happy to show you her facility. Ask her what titles her dogs have won. She should be able to show you ribbons and photos of dogs she has shown in obedience shows and other areas.

The trainer should use positive techniques to train the dogs. There should be very little, if any, harsh commands or corrections. Instead, you should see effective training techniques that train the owner to train the dog.

Nowadays most trainers use positive reinforcement training, but there are still some who use harsh techniques from over 20 years ago. In most cases, these techniques are antiquated.

Lab Bites

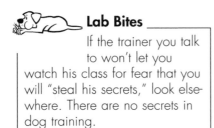

If the trainer you talk to won't let you watch his class for fear that you will "steal his secrets," look elsewhere. There are no secrets in dog training.

Training Classes Explained

Most facilities have a variety of training classes available. Many will teach basic obedience geared toward the beginner; however, there may be classes for competitive obedience.

Puppy Kindergarten

Puppy Kindergarten, also called Puppy KPT, is for puppies under the age of six months. In these classes, you socialize your Lab with other puppies of about the same age. The trainer will also help you teach your puppy fundamental commands such as Sit and Down. These classes generally run an hour once a week for five or six weeks.

Beginning Obedience

Beginning Obedience usually starts where Puppy Kindergarten leaves off. In Beginning Obedience, the trainer teaches the owner to train the dog to do the basic commands:

- Sit
- Down
- Heel
- Stay
- Stand
- Come

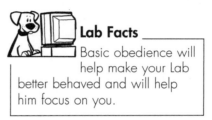

> **Lab Facts**
> Basic obedience will help make your Lab better behaved and will help him focus on you.

Sometimes this class is similar to a Novice Competitive class (see the following section), but this class is intended for training dogs with no experience in obedience and no intention to compete.

Novice Competitive

Novice Competitive class is aimed toward owners who want to compete in obedience competition. Those who compete in Novice competition must pass three trials consisting of several tests. In Novice Competitive class, the owner learns the commands that make up the basic test for Novice:

- Heeling on leash—the dog heels on the leash in a pattern
- Figure eights—the dog heels in a figure-8 pattern
- Sit
- Down
- Stand-stay—the dog must stay in a standing position while he is examined by the judge
- Down-stay—the dog must stay in the down for three minutes

- Sit-stay—the dog must sit for a minute
- Front—the dog must come to the handler and stand in front
- Finish—the dog must return to the heel position

Other Classes

Other classes are usually advanced obedience classes, such as open and excellent training, which your Lab can progress to after Novice. However, some trainers may have a *clicker training* class, attention class, and beginning tracking.

Clicker training is a fun class in which you click a special clicker every time your Lab does something you want. You follow up the click with a treat. Most dogs (and owners) love clicker training because it is very positive. Clicker training can be started at any time in your Lab's training. You can use it with basic obedience, if you'd like.

Attention class helps the dog focus on the owner. Most Labs don't need attention class because they are people-oriented dogs. However, if your Lab is having dominance problems or needs an "edge" in competition, often this class will help him focus on you. This class can help dogs who are easily distracted by other dogs and activities outside of the home.

Lab Lingo

Clicker training—A form of positive reinforcement that relies heavily on operant conditioning. When he does something right, the dog hears a click from a special clicker and is conditioned to expect a treat. Dogs quickly learn to do things that will cause the click (and the subsequent treat) and avoid behaviors that will not produce the click.

Agility—A sport where dogs go through a specially designed obstacle course. It is a timed event, so dogs who complete the course accurately in the least amount of time do well.

Stack—Standing one's dog in the conformation show ring to emphasize positive characteristics and diminish flaws.

Tracking class teaches your Lab to follow his nose and find items with scent on them, known as "articles." Tracking is a lot of fun for both the dog and owner, but requires some obedience training first.

Take Your Training Further: Competitive Dog Sports

Obedience isn't the only thing you can do with your Lab. There are sports where you can show off your Lab. You can compete in conformation (dog shows), agility trials, and even hunting tests. See Chapter 11 for more information on dog sports.

Agility

Agility is a sport where dogs go through a specially designed obstacle course. It is a timed event, so dogs who complete the course accurately in the least amount of time do well. Most dogs love agility once they get the hang of the obstacles. Dogs who might not do well in obedience may shine in agility because it isn't as repetitive. Your Lab will need to know basic obedience commands such as Sit, Down, Come, and Stay, and must be able to work off the leash.

Lab Facts

Agility is a fast-growing sport. Sanctioning bodies include the AKC, the UKC (United Kennel Club), the NADAC (North American Dog Agility Council), and the USDAA (United States Dog Agility Association). Each has its own version of agility competition that your Lab can compete in.

Conformation

Conformation training is training for a conformation dog show. In this class, the trainer teaches you how to *stack* your Lab so that he looks his best when the judge sees him. You also learn how to handle a dog properly for the show ring and how to "gait him"—trot him to show off his movement to the best advantage.

Lab Facts

Your Lab can earn a variety of titles through the AKC and other organizations. The following is a partial list of titles that are available:

Sport	Title
Conformation	Champion (CH)
Obedience	Companion Dog (CD)
	Companion Dog Excellent (CDX)
	Utility Dog (UD)
	Utility Dog Excellent (UDX)
	Obedience Trial Champion (OTCH)
	Canine Good Citizen (CGC)
Hunting Test	Junior Hunter (JH)
	Senior Hunter (SH)
	Master Hunter (MH)
Field Trial	Field Champion (FC)
	National Field Trial Champion (NFC)
	Amateur Field Trial Champion (AFC)
	National Amateur Field Trial Champion (NAFC)
Tracking	Tracking Dog (TD)
	Tracking Dog Excellent (TDX)
	Variable Surface Tracking Dog (VST)
	Champion Tracker (CT) (has earned all three of the above)
Agility	Novice Agility (NA)
	Novice Jumpers with Weaves (NAJ)
	Open Agility (OA)
	Open Jumpers with Weaves (OAJ)
	Excellent Jumpers with Weaves (AXJ)
	Agility Excellent (AX)
	Master Agility Excellent (MX)
	Master Jumpers with Weaves (MXJ)
	Master Agility Champion (MACH)

Field Trial/Hunting Tests/Retrieving Work

Field Trial and Hunting Tests training introduce or prepare the Lab for competition in either Field Trial Competition or Hunting Tests. Field Trial competition is very competitive, so if you're interested in trying out some form of field work or hunting, check out hunting tests. The main difference between hunt tests and field trials is that the hunt test program is noncompetitive. Dogs either pass and receive a qualifying score and credit toward a title, or they fail. The distances of the marks and blinds are also much shorter than at field trials. The handlers carry guns and wear camouflage, too—in other words, hunt tests are less competitive and are more like real hunting.

Lab Facts

Your Lab can earn titles in obedience, tracking, conformation, and hunting tests. Only conformation and field trials require the dog to be "intact." All other competition allows spayed or neutered dogs to compete.

The Least You Need to Know

- You are more likely to be successful teaching your Lab obedience if you learn under a professional trainer.
- Ask your vet, your Lab's breeder, or a dog-owning friend whom they would recommend as a professional dog trainer. Choose a trainer who uses positive reinforcement techniques and teaches you to train your dog.
- Young puppies (under six months) should go to a Puppy Kindergarten class. Older puppies and dogs should take a beginner's obedience class.
- More advanced classes teach sports such as agility, tracking, conformation, field, and retrieving work. Most require that the dog have some basic obedience.

Obedience Training

In This Chapter

- Necessary training equipment, including the best leashes and collars
- The basic commands: Sit, Down, Stay, Okay, Come, and Heel, as well as walking on a leash nicely
- Other useful commands: Drop, Off, and Leave it!
- The secrets of professional trainers

Obedience training makes the difference between an enjoyable Lab and one who is out of control. In this chapter, we start with a rundown of the best training equipment to have. Then we cover the basic commands every Lab should know. This includes Sit, Down, Stay, Okay, Come, and Heel.

But there are other commands you should teach your Lab. These include Drop, Off, and Leave it! We'll also show you how to walk down the street with your Lab instead of being dragged.

Collars

Lab should have a training collar as well as his regular (flat or buckled) collar. Use the training collar only for training. Most training collars act like a slip collar, meaning that they tighten up as you pull on them. If you leave a slip collar on all the time—even one with limited slip—your Lab may snag it on something and choke to death. For this reason, never leave a slip or limited-slip collar on an unattended dog. Never affix to the training collar tags or anything that may snag, other than the leash or training tab. There are other types of training collars, namely prong or pinch collars, snap chokes, and head halters. These should be used only under the guidance of a professional trainer. Use a collar with the minimal amount of correction first before stepping up to firmer collars such as the snap choke or prong. Most people work with a flat collar first and may change over to a slip or *limited-slip collar.*

The Slip Collar

The *slip collar* is another name for what people commonly refer to as the "choke chain" or "choke collar." This name conjures up some cruel images. But in fact, if you use the collar correctly, it can be a safe and humane training collar.

These collars may be made from steel chain (for regular obedience), fine serpentine links (for dog shows), or nylon cord. Depending on your activities, you may want several types of training collars.

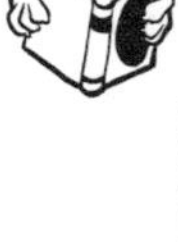

Lab Lingo

Slip collar—A collar used for training purposes, usually made from chain. This collar tightens when you pull on it.

Limited-slip collar—A slip collar that has a restriction that prevents the collar from tightening too much.

Choose a steel-link training collar. There should be no slack or ends dangling down. The collar should fit around your Lab's neck, high enough so that it sits below the jaw and just behind the ears. Labs have notoriously strong necks. If you allow the collar to rest on those thick muscles, you may find yourself going for a "drag" instead of a walk! Consult a professional trainer for the proper fit if you're unfamiliar with the fit of a training collar.

Lab Bites

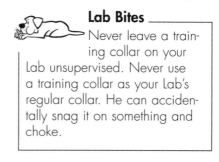

Never leave a training collar on your Lab unsupervised. Never use a training collar as your Lab's regular collar. He can accidentally snag it on something and choke.

There's a right way and a wrong way to put on a training collar. The correct way allows the collar to release after tightening; the wrong way keeps the collar tight. Slide one link through the other so that the collar makes a "P." Slip the collar over your Lab's head as your Lab is facing you. If the collar is a backward "P," it is on wrong.

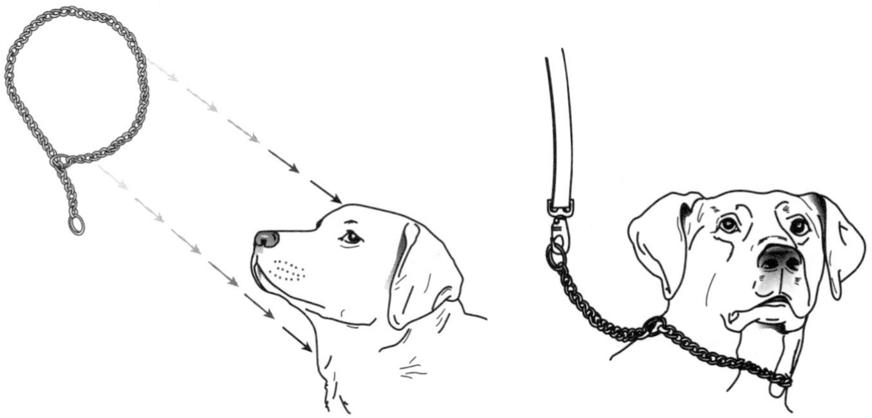

The proper way to fit a training collar. Slide one link through the other so that the collar makes a "P." Slip the collar over your Lab's head as he is facing you. If the collar is a backward "P," it's on wrong.

In most circumstances, Labs do well with slip collars, however, if you are constantly getting dragged around by your Lab, you may have to resort to a firmer collar such as a *snap choke* or a *prong collar*.

The Prong Collar

Prong collars look like medieval torture devices, but are actually quite humane. They are sometimes called "pinch" collars because the prongs close on the neck's skin folds. These collars have limited slip, thus making them safer than slip collars. But the prongs can do damage if the dog slips and falls.

Prong collars work best for extremely strong dogs with thick, muscular necks who pull like last year's Iditarod champions. Because these collars don't work by tightening like standard slip collars, there is less chance of damaging your Lab's neck. However, like any tool, it can be misused. Consult a professional trainer on using a prong collar.

Once your Lab learns to stop pulling, most trainers graduate their dogs to snap chokes or regular slip collars. Most dogs make the transition well, needing the prong collar only as an occasional reminder or in circumstances that require tight control.

Lab Lingo

Prong collar—A collar, used for training purposes, made from steel links with prongs that turn inside against the dog's neck. This collar has a limited-slip design. When pulled, it will cause the prongs to grab into the loose folds of skin around the dog's neck.

Snap choke—A type of slip collar that snaps onto a loose ring. It is made of parachute cord rather than steel links and offers more control than the standard slip collar.

The Snap Choke Collar

Snap chokes are very similar to slip collars, except that they are made from very thin parachute cord and snap onto a loose ring. You can get a better fit with a snap choke than you can with regular training collars. Like regular training collars, they need to fit close around the neck with no excess hanging down.

These training collars are very effective for strong pullers, but are less effective than prong collars. Like prong collars, they can be misused, so consult a professional trainer in the proper use of snap chokes.

The Head Halter

Head halters are a popular device among those who don't wish to use training collars. The head halter works like a horse halter, although it has some differences. You clip the leash onto the strap hanging down. The strap will apply pressure on the dog's muzzle when pulled.

Many people swear by these halters, but I've seen mixed results. The control is marginal when compared to a properly obedience-trained dog. Dog's heads come in all shapes and sizes and your Lab may be clever enough to slip out of one. Some dogs will toss their heads back and forth, risking neck injury. Dogs who are prone to overheating (particularly black dogs) may have their airflow restricted and may be in greater danger of overheating. Lastly, these halters look like muzzles and may give a very bad impression of your Lab. AKC dog shows don't allow head halters. So if you train with one, you will also have to train with a regular training collar.

Leashes and Other Equipment

There are a variety of leashes available including nylon, leather, cotton, retractable-type leashes, leashes made from mountain climbing rope, and others. When you look for a training leash, it should be a six-foot latigo leather leash.

Latigo Leather Leashes

Why a latigo leather leash? They're expensive, certainly, but well worth the money. Quite simply, your hands will thank me. If your Lab pulls at all on his leash—and many do—a leash made from nylon or other materials will cut into your hands. Leather is remarkably strong, but it is tasty, so keep it out of reach.

When I first got into dogs, I used the traditional nylon leash. The trainer showed me the error of my ways and told me to switch to a leather leash. All of a sudden, my dogs began paying attention to me and my hands stopped hurting. Save the nylon leashes for when your Lab is a perfect heeler—buy a leather leash now.

> **Retriever Rewards**
>
> Purchase a six-foot latigo leather leash as your Lab's training leash. Your hands will thank me! Leashes made from other materials will cut into your hands. And retractable leashes usually offer little control with big dogs like Labs.

What about those retractable leads? They are useful to train the Come command, but usually aren't strong enough for a big dog like a Lab. Likewise, you will have very little control with them.

Long Lines (Tracking Leads)

Long lines are long leashes (usually called *tracking leads*) used for training. You'll want at least a tracking lead or a retractable lead for working on commands such as Come.

Clicker

This is a special device used in clicker training. It's a small, rectangular box that has a strip of thin metal inside. You press on the metal strip to make a definite click noise. If you plan on clicker training, you'll need several of these (you can lose them).

Lab Lingo

Tracking leads—Leashes made from cotton or nylon that can be anywhere from 10 to 30 feet in length. Trainers use these leads for tracking work (hence the name) but also for distance work such as working on the Recall command.

Bait pouches—Little pouches that allow you to carry your treats if you don't have pockets or if you don't want to get your pockets messy. They're called "bait" because when you stack a dog in conformation, you lure or "bait" him with a treat so that he will look attentive.

Bait Pouches

Bait pouches are little pouches that allow you to carry your treats if you don't have pockets or if you don't want to get your pockets messy. The AKC allows bait pouches in conformation dog shows, but not in obedience, agility, or other forms of performance competition.

Treats

Treats should be anything your Lab likes. Some people use dog biscuits or other doggy snacks, but many trainers offer bits of hot dog, cheese, cooked bacon, cold cuts, liver, and other enticing items. The treat should be small enough to give your Lab just a "taste." You will be giving him many treats when you train. You don't want him to get fat!

Retriever Rewards

Some treat manufacturers make small treats expressly for training purposes. These are handy if you run out of cheese or hot dogs.

Start Training the Basic Commands

So, now that you have all the equipment you'll need, how do you start training your Lab? This section discusses the basic commands that all dogs should know.

Walk Nicely on the Leash

The first step is to get your Lab to walk nicely on the leash. After all, you don't want him forging ahead or wrapping around you. Put on your Lab's training collar, put a handful of treats in your pocket, and clip his leash to his training collar.

Retriever Rewards

Always be happy and upbeat when training your Lab. You'll both look forward to the training sessions together.

Your Lab may pull, whirl around, or just stand there. Use a treat to lure your Lab into a position where the collar is no longer tight around his neck. Give him the treat and gentle praise. If he struggles against the collar, try clipping his leash to his flat collar. (Be certain that the flat collar is tight enough so he can't slip out!)

Once your Lab has calmed sufficiently, bring him outside. Let him get used to the leash and the upward pull on his own terms. Usually there's something interesting outside and he will lose his apprehension over the leash.

Lab Facts

You can start your Lab with the clicker easily. Click the clicker and then give him a treat. Do this several times so that he starts noticing that he receives a treat every time he hears a click.

Now, when you click, toss the treat in various places around your Lab. He will learn that the treat may appear in different places, but he still will associate it with the click.

Vary the time between the click and the treat, so that your Lab learns he will get a treat even after a certain amount of time has passed.

Once your Lab is used to associating clicks with treats, you can now associate the clicks with his actions. Let's say your Lab sits down. Click and give him a treat. Now your Lab may associate that sit with the click and subsequent treat.

Once your Lab becomes used to the leash, he may start pulling or try to tangle. You can use either the clicker or praise to tell him when he is doing the right thing. Use treats to lure him back to where he is no longer pulling and give him plenty of treats and praise.

(© Jacky Sachs)

Always reward your Lab for coming to you.

Sit

Have your Lab on a loose leash. Take a treat and hold it over his nose. Bring the treat backward while gently pushing on your Lab's rear. Say, "Buddy, Sit!"

Most Labs will sit. Give him the treat and praise him. You'll need to practice this a few times before your Lab will learn it.

Once your Lab learns Sit, don't use the treat as a lure anymore. Instead, give him the treat once he is in Sit. Then you can give your Lab the treat occasionally when he performs a Sit.

Down

Have your Lab sit while on a loose leash. Take a treat and lower it from his nose to the ground, close to your Lab's chest. Say, "Buddy, Down!" Most Labs will follow the treat to the ground.

He may need a little help to complete the down. If so, gently push on his shoulders. Give him praise and a treat when he is in the down position. As with Sit, you will need to practice this a few times before your Lab learns it.

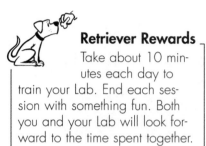

> **Retriever Rewards**
>
> Take about 10 minutes each day to train your Lab. End each session with something fun. Both you and your Lab will look forward to the time spent together.

Once your Lab learns Down, don't use the treat as a lure anymore. Instead, give him the treat once he is in Down. Then you can give your Lab the treat occasionally when he performs a Down.

Stay

Many dogs find Stay more difficult to learn than other commands. Your Lab should know Sit or Down well enough before proceeding to Stay. Put your Lab in the Sit or Down position. Now, with a sweeping gesture of your open palm, bring your hand in front of your Lab's face and say, "Buddy, Stay!" Take a step (right foot first) or two and turn around.

Your Lab may try to follow you. If so, say "No, Buddy, Stay!" and put him back in his original Stay position. When you get him to stay for a few seconds, release him with an "Okay" and then praise him and give him a treat.

Increase the time by giving him a treat while he is in the Stay position. Wait a few seconds, and then go back and give your Lab a treat. Quietly praise him: "Good stay!" If he stands up, gently put him back in the Stay position. You can gradually increase your Lab's time in the Stay.

Increase the time between giving your Lab treats once he has learned Stay. Eventually, you'll be giving him a treat after he completes a Stay.

(© Kent and Donna Dammen)

When your Lab is obedience trained, it makes outings much more enjoyable.

Don't get angry if your Lab breaks his stay. Simply put him back in Stay. You don't want your Lab to break his stay because he is apprehensive or fearful.

You can increase time or distance while practicing Stay with your Lab, but not both. If your Lab breaks his stay, start with short intervals and short distances away from your Lab and work your way up. Don't increase the time or distance until your Lab is reliably staying at the current time and distance.

You can practice Sit-stay and Down-stay at home easily. Put your Lab in a Sit-stay while you are fixing his dinner or put him in a Down-stay while you are watching television.

Okay: The Release Word

"Okay" is a generic release word that trainers use to let the dog know he can leave his stay. You can use Okay to let your Lab know that a particular training exercise is done or that he doesn't have to *heel* any longer.

> **Lab Lingo**
> **Heel position**—A position where your dog sits or stands beside your left side, right next to your knee.

Most dogs learn Okay faster than the commands they're being released from. To teach Okay, simply put your Lab in a Down-stay or Sit-stay. When you release him with an "Okay," make a big fuss—as if he were the best dog in the world. Your Lab will catch on quickly.

Come

Come is a vital command for your Lab to learn. Unfortunately, too many dogs don't have a reliable recall. This can be dangerous, if not deadly. A dog who won't come when you call him can be hit by a car or may take off into the wilderness. Don't let this happen!

Start by teaching your Lab that good things happen when you call him. Give him a treat every time he comes to you. Always praise your Lab for coming and never call your Lab to you when you correct him—always go to him.

> **Lab Bites**
> Never call your Lab to you to punish him. If you must give a correction, go to your Lab. When you call your Lab to you for a correction, you've just punished your Lab for coming to you—not for the transgression!

Start training Come in an enclosed area. You'll need the six-foot leash. Clip the leash to your Lab's collar. Put your Lab in Sit-stay and walk out to the end of the leash and turn around. Say, "Buddy, come!" in a happy, upbeat tone.

If you've been practicing Come with treats, your Lab will probably come right to you. Give him a treat and praise him for being such a good boy! If you haven't been practicing Come or if your Lab sits and looks at you as though you were a space alien, try again, this time more enthusiastic and upbeat. You may want to tug lightly on the leash so that he gets the idea he should come to you.

Once your Lab comes, praise him and give him treats as though he has done the most marvelous thing in the universe. Now, put him in Sit-stay again and walk out to the end of his leash. Be careful that he doesn't break his stay in his enthusiasm to come to you. If he does, tell him "No, stay," and put him back in his Sit-stay. Don't sound angry when you do this, just be matter-of-fact. Then tell him to come again.

Practice Come at short distances. Then gradually lengthen the distance with a long-line or retractable leash. When you call your Lab, either retract the leash or reel in the long-line quickly. If at any time your Lab fails to come directly to you, return to shorter distances.

Retriever Rewards

Retractable leashes are wonderful for teaching Come. When you put your Lab in a Sit-stay, feed out as much line as you'll need for the recall and then lock it in place. Then, go to the spot you intend to call him, give your command to come, and release the line so that it retracts.

Once you think your Lab is reliable coming to you on the leash, try adding distractions. A busy park is a good place to practice. Start with a six-foot leash and practice recalls as though you were just starting out.

Your Lab may be too excited by all the new things to pay attention to you. Try using treats to focus his attention on you rather than the distractions. If six feet is too far, work with him at a shorter distance. Then gradually increase the distance.

Lab Bites

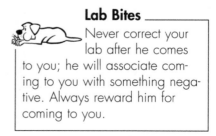

Never correct your lab after he comes to you; he will associate coming to you with something negative. Always reward him for coming to you.

Eventually, you will want to practice off-leash recalls. When you do practice, find an enclosed area such as your backyard, a dog training area at a local park, or maybe an enclosed baseball diamond or tennis court.

If at any time your Lab takes off or ignores you, it's time to go back to the beginning and work on basic recall training.

Heeling on Leash

Heeling on leash starts with learning the heel position. Teach your Lab the Heel position by luring him to your left side with a treat. When he stands or sits at your left side, give him a treat. Use a one-word command such as Heel or Place.

Once your Lab has learned the Heel position, clip the leash on his training collar. You should hold the leash loosely in your left hand with any excess leash in your right hand.

Hold a treat in your left hand. Say, "Buddy, heel," and start walking, left foot forward. If your Lab forges ahead, lags behind, or moves out of the Heel position, use the treat to lure him back to the Heel position. When you stop, put your Lab in a sit and give him a treat. You can then slowly wean your dog off treats by giving him a treat only when he sits and then slowly reduce the times you give a treat.

Lab Facts

Why worry about which foot to use for Stay versus Heel? Dogs, especially Labs, are keen observers and will notice which foot you use when you say, "Stay" versus "Heel." The left foot is closest to your Lab when you heel, so he will see that movement first.

When you put your Lab in stay, do so on your left side and leave with the *right* foot first. Your Lab won't see the movement right away and it will be an extra signal to stay.

Other Useful Commands

There are other commands you may find useful for training your Lab, although you won't find them used in competitive obedience. These commands help reshape your Lab's behavior—teaching him proper behavior in place of negative actions. Other commands will help teach your Lab what you want him to do. You may add more words to your Lab's repertoire as required, but the basic commands are Off, Drop, Leave it!, Watch me!, Out, and Bed.

Retriever Rewards

Dogs can learn many different words and commands and aren't limited to just obedience commands. Your Lab will pick up on certain words such as "walk," "biscuit," "snack," "out," or "bed." Use these key words or phrases to communicate with your Lab.

Most of these commands are easy to teach—you may accidentally teach your Lab these commands without knowing you've done it! I've accidentally taught my dogs "Oops!" That means, "I'm clumsy and I just dropped something." Usually that something is food and my dogs know now that when I say "Oops," they should look on the floor for tidbits.

The Off Command

Off is a command meaning "all four paws on the floor, please!" Use this command whenever you mean "get down from that!" You can use this command when your Lab jumps up on you. When he does, tell him "Off!" and push him down so that all four feet are on the ground. Then give him a treat. You can also use Off when your Lab has sneaked up on the couch or some other forbidden piece of furniture.

The Drop or Trade Command

Labs are exquisite food thieves. The problem is that what smells yummy to Labs may not be in their best interest. If your Lab isn't possessive of food, you may be able to teach him to "drop it."

You can teach this command by gently squeezing open your Lab's jaws by applying gentle but consistent pressure with your fingers where the upper and lower jaws meet. Once your Lab opens his mouth, say, "Drop it," and allow the item to fall from his mouth. Give him a treat for being a good dog and take the items away.

If your Lab's jaws are too strong or you're afraid of getting bit, there is an alternative method. Say, "Trade!" and offer a treat that is better than what your Lab has in his mouth. Your Lab will usually drop the item for something more tasty.

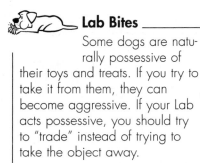

> **Lab Bites**
>
> Some dogs are naturally possessive of their toys and treats. If you try to take it from them, they can become aggressive. If your Lab acts possessive, you should try to "trade" instead of trying to take the object away.

You can practice Trade easily. When your Lab is chewing on a rawhide or playing with a toy, offer to "trade" with something yummy. When your Lab drops the toy for your treat, take the toy and give your Lab the treat at the same time.

The Leave It! Command

Leave it! is a command that tells your Lab to leave alone whatever interests him. Usually this is something you do along with a short snap of the collar. However, you can also combine it with a Watch me! command.

The Watch Me! Command

You can use Watch me! to make your Lab pay attention to you rather than something else. Start by showing your Lab a treat and bringing the treat up to your face. Tell him, "Watch me!" Give your Lab the treat once he makes eye contact.

The Out Command

You can tell your Lab when to go to the door to go outside by associating the word *out* with it. When you walk your Lab or let him outside in the backyard, simply say "Out!" It won't take long before he learns what Out means.

The Bed Command

Bed is another command most Labs learn by association. When you tell your Lab to go to his bed or crate, he learns quickly what his bed is. You can teach your Lab to go into his crate easily by tossing a treat into it and telling him "Bed."

Secrets of Professional Trainers—Do's and Don'ts

Professional trainers know the secrets to training dogs. Now you can learn the same techniques they know. These tips will help your Lab learn faster and make you look like a pro.

- **Don't yell and scream when your Lab does something wrong.** You haven't corrected him—you've just made him afraid of you.
- **Corrections and praise should be swift and meaningful to the dog.** The correction must match the action. Don't take away your dog's dinner because he broke a Sit-stay—the punishment is meaningless to the dog. Instead, put your Lab back in the Sit-stay.
- **Spend 5 to 10 minutes a day working on commands.**
- **Don't wheedle and cajole your Lab to obey a command.** Don't repeat yourself except when teaching a new command.

Repeating the command teaches your dog to count and not to obey the command.

- **Never get angry at your Lab.** If you feel yourself becoming angry or frustrated—stop. Take a time out. Stop training. Don't take your frustration out on your dog.
- **Become a person your dog will respect.** Be fair and consistent.
- **Never give a command that you cannot enforce.** That one time is when your Lab won't obey and then he will always remember that he got away with it. Enforce all commands.
- **Always set your Lab up for success and never allow him to make a mistake.** When you start training your Lab, think up all the possible reactions and account for the possibilities. Then guide your Lab into the correct action.
- **Train before meals.** You know how sleepy you are after you eat a big dinner—your Lab is less alert after eating, too. Dinner can also be an added reward for a job well done.
- **Always reward your dog for coming to you.** Never punish a dog when he runs away and then comes back or you will be punishing the dog for coming back.
- **Never force a frightened or confused dog to do something.** You will most likely be bitten.
- **Teach your dog to pay attention to you.** You can do so with food and the Watch me! command.
- **Before you can teach a command, you must first have your dog's attention.** Always precede the command with your dog's name, such as "Buddy, come!" Don't say, "Come, Buddy!" Buddy is likely to have not heard the command before you got his attention.
- **Choose one command word for each action, and stick with it.**

(Photo courtesy Canine Companions for Independence)

Your Lab will enjoy the chance to feel useful. It all starts with basic obedience.

- **Never call your Lab to you to punish him.** If you must give a correction, go to your Lab.
- **Choose one-word commands that don't sound like each other.** Sit down and Lie down are perfect examples of what will confuse your Lab. Use Sit for Sit down and Down for Lie down.
- **Don't use Down for Off.** Down should mean lie down. Off should mean four paws on the ground.
- **Always reward good behavior.**
- **It is easier to teach good habits than to unlearn bad ones.** Don't allow your Lab to learn bad behavior by preventing it.
- **Never allow a puppy to do something you do not want her to do as an adult.** Mouthing turns to biting. Jumping up turns to knocking over. Correct bad habits before they can become ingrained.

Lab Bites

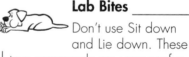

Don't use Sit down and Lie down. These two commands are very confusing. Instead, use Sit for Sit down and Down for Lie down.

Retriever Rewards

If basic obedience is a breeze for you and your Lab, you might consider competetive obedience. In competetive obedience, you're judged on how well your lab performs in the ring.

- **Always end a training session on a positive note.** If your Lab isn't doing well during this session, find something that she can do and end on success.
- **Have fun.** Take time to play. Play with your Lab after the training session.

The Least You Need to Know

- The minimum equipment you'll need for training is a training collar (usually a slip collar), a six-foot leather leash, and treats. Other useful items include clickers and long lines.
- The very basic commands are Sit, Down, Stay, Okay, Come, and Heel.
- Your Lab may need to learn other commands such as Off, Drop, Leave it!, Watch me!, Out, and Bed.
- The basic do's and don'ts of obedience training include positive reinforcement, consistency, clarity, and patience.

Chapter 11

Advanced Training for Dog Sports

In This Chapter

- What is conformation?
- Tracking training
- Agility training
- Teach your Labrador Retriever how to retrieve

Labrador Retrievers are the quintessential do-it-all dogs. Perhaps you'd like to take advantage of your Lab's talents and work in sports that show what a very special dog he is.

In this chapter, you'll learn the various sporting activities you can do with your Lab. These run the gamut from conformation, tracking, and agility to hunting and retrieving.

Whatever you decide to try, Labs can become stars in any of these activities. You'll have a lot of fun and spend time with your best friend.

What Is Conformation?

Conformation is the quintessential "dog show." At a conformation show, judges evaluate the dogs on how well they conform to the standard for their breed. Dog shows are intended for purebred dogs, but not every purebred dog should be shown at a dog show. Indeed, most dogs—including most Labrador Retrievers—are pet quality. This means that the dog has a superficial "fault" that precludes her from conforming to standard.

This certainly doesn't mean the dog is any less of a pet. Indeed, many Labs who aren't show quality do exceptionally well in other venues such as retrieving, obedience, agility, and search and rescue.

Judges from around the country come to dog shows to judge dogs based on their breed standards. Judges choose dogs who conform closest to the standard. Dogs who have not already become champions vie for *points* toward their championship. A dog may earn up to 5 points in a show. The amount of points won depends largely on the number of entrants for that breed. If the points are 3 or more, the dog is said to have won a *major*. Once your Lab earns his 15 points, he is a Champion and will have a "Ch." before his name. Champion dogs may still compete for Best of Breed and Best in Show titles along with other competitors.

Lab Facts

Show-quality Labs are shown as breeding stock; thus they must not have been spayed or neutered. You can show neutered and spayed Labs only in Veteran's classes.

Grooming for Conformation

Unlike Poodles or other dogs with high-maintenance coats, preparing the Labrador Retriever for the show ring is a breeze. You must wash your Lab, comb him out, and clip his toenails. That's pretty much it. No wonder Labs are the quintessential wash-and-wear dogs!

Training for Conformation

If only training for conformation were as easy as grooming your Labrador Retriever. There are whole books written on the subject of showing dogs. The best way to train is to find a conformation class near you and work with your Lab. You may also want to find a "mentor"—someone who will "show you the ropes" in conformation. It's difficult to learn handling from a book without taking a class or practicing it yourself.

Retriever Rewards

Find a mentor who will help you train in conformation. He or she can show you tricks in handling and can evaluate what you're doing wrong or right.

Lab Facts

After your Lab earns 15 points—which must include two majors under two separate judges—he is a Champion and will have a "Ch." before his name.

In the ring, the judge has the handlers gait their Labs once around the ring. The judge then considers each individual dog, looking at his or her face and bite, and feeling down the forelegs, back, and rear legs. On males, the judge will feel the testicles to determine whether the dog is intact and has fully descended testicles. The judge will ask the handler to gait the Lab in a pattern: up and back, L-shaped, or triangle-shaped. The judge will then ask the handler to gait the Lab to the rear of the line.

Training for the ring requires that the handler "stack" the dog. Stacking refers to standing your Lab straight on all fours to emphasize his positive aspects and hide flaws that might penalize him. You must also bait your Lab with food or treats to produce an attentive expression.

Tracking

Does the nose know? Is your Labrador a Bloodhound in disguise? Maybe you and your Lab will have fun tracking down items and people. The AKC offers tracking titles for purebred dogs, including the Labrador Retriever.

Lab Lingo

Track—The tracking "course" where the dogs follow the scent that the track layer has laid down.

Leg—In tracking, a distinct segment of the course.

Article—An item impregnated with scent and used for tracking.

Training for Tracking

Training your Lab for tracking is somewhat complex. Most people start out in a tracking course after their Lab has learned obedience. You should probably look for a professional trainer who teaches tracking and enroll in a tracking course.

Retriever Rewards

You'll need specialized equipment for tracking. This equipment includes the following:

- **Tracking Harness**—A walking harness that won't restrict movement.
- **Tracking Lead**—A long leash between 20 and 40 feet long (AKC regulation). You may want a slightly shorter leash for training, for more control.
- **Scent or Tracking Articles**—Leather gloves or wallets used for scent training. You'll need other articles later as your Labrador becomes more proficient in tracking.

Most trainers start with a single article, usually a leather glove. To start training your dog to track, follow these steps:

1. Show your Lab the glove and tease him with it; encourage him to recognize that it is something desirable to find. Let him play with it and encourage him to find it.

2. Put treats in it so that he associates the glove with fun and tasty things.
3. Next, put your Lab in a Sit-stay, fill the glove with treats, walk in a straight line away from him, and drop the glove about 10 feet away from him.
4. Return to your Lab and tell him "Find!" If you've trained him to think of the glove as his toy, he'll race to grab the glove and the treats. If he doesn't, lead him to the glove.
5. Praise him and give him the treats when he "finds" the glove.
6. Practice this often in the same place until your Lab races to get the glove.

Retriever Rewards

Make your tracking sessions short and fun—no more than 15 minutes a day. This is hard work for your Lab! End each tracking session with playtime. You'll both look forward to training together.

(© Kent and Donna Dannen)

This Lab is tracking a scent.

Alternatively, you can use the "Hansel and Gretel" approach; that is, leave a trail of treats to the glove. This way, you're teaching your Lab to keep his nose down to sniff for the scent.

Next, switch locations, not far from where you practiced finding the glove the first time. If your Lab is pretty savvy, he'll watch to see where you put the glove and race to it. However, some are a little slow on the uptake, so don't be surprised if your Lab runs to the first spot and looks for the glove there. If he does, just show him the new spot.

> **Lab Facts**
>
> The AKC has four titles for dogs competing in tracking:
>
> Tracking Dog (TD)
>
> Tracking Dog Excellent (TDX)
>
> Variable Surface Tracking (VST)
>
> Champion Tracker (CT)

As you keep switching the location, you may have to try the "Hansel and Gretel" method. The main thing is to keep him looking for the glove and give him treats when he finds it.

When your Lab is comfortable looking for the glove, put him in a place where he cannot see you "hide" it. Make a short track, drop the glove, and then walk back along that same track. The track should be no more than 10 feet. Bring him to the start of the track and tell him "Find!" Your Lab may be confused at first. If necessary, help him find the glove or line the trail with treats. When he finds the glove, give him praise and treats!

Agility

Maybe your Lab is a superstar athlete, full of energy. If so, maybe agility is more to your liking. What is agility? It's one of the fastest growing dog sports. Dogs compete on an obstacle course where they must climb over dog walks, through tunnels, over jumps, and through weave poles. It's exciting to watch and even more fun to participate.

(© Kent and Donna Dannen)

Labs are exceptional in agility. This Lab is weaving through weave poles on an agility course.

Lab Lingo

Contact obstacles—A contact obstacle is an agility obstacle that the dog must climb up on and travel across—that is, make contact with. Contact obstacles frequently have zones that the dog must touch to avoid disqualification.

Relay—A type of agility course where a team runs the course in relays.

Agility Obstacles

The first step to training in agility is getting your Lab used to the obstacles. The agility obstacles vary depending on which organization sponsors the competition, but there are a number of basic obstacles that are common:

- **A-frame**—A contact obstacle, the A-frame is two 6 to 9-foot ramps that meet in a peak at the center and are 3 to 4 feet wide. Your Lab must climb the A-frame to the peak and then climb down it, touching the contact areas on the way down.

- **Dogwalk**—A contact obstacle, the dogwalk is a single plank connected by two ramps. It is a tall obstacle, similar to a "catwalk." Your Lab must climb up the dogwalk, cross the plank, and descend the ramp, touching contacts on both sides.
- **Seesaw**—A contact obstacle, the seesaw looks like a playground teeter-totter without the handlebars. Your Lab enters the seesaw on the downside, crosses the seesaw, and tips the plank. Your Lab must touch the contact zones on both sides.
- **Table**—Although the dog steps on the table, it isn't considered a true contact obstacle. It is a square table that looks like a large end table that can be set to the various jump heights. Your Lab must hop on the table and sit or lie down on it, depending on the command.
- **Hurdles**—There are a variety of jumps, with or without side wings, that your Lab may have to jump.
- **Tire jump**—This is a jump in the shape of a tire. Surprisingly, the tire is difficult for dogs because they must jump through instead of over.

Lab Lingo

Off-course—In agility, a dog incurs an off-course penalty if he takes the wrong obstacle in the sequence or enters the obstacle from the wrong side.

Refusal—In agility, a dog incurs a refusal penalty (in AKC competitions only) if he passes the obstacle or heads toward the obstacle and then turns away.

Lab Bites

When your Lab learns the obstacles, it's tempting to think that you're both ready for your first agility trial. Nothing could be farther from the truth! The next step is learning how to sequence—that is, how to properly put the obstacles together into a clean run (a run without faults). If you're interested in learning more about agility, I've written a book on the very subject called *An Introduction to Dog Agility*. Check out the bibliography for specifics.

- **Pipe tunnel or open tunnel**—The pipe tunnel is a tunnel that can snake into various patterns. Most dogs love tunnels and your Lab will enjoy this fun obstacle.
- **Closed tunnel**—The closed tunnel has an opening at one end (usually a barrel) with an 8 to 12 foot long "chute" made of silk or parachute cloth that lays flat at the other end. Your Lab will have to enter the open side of the closed tunnel and push his way through the chute to complete the obstacle.
- **Weave poles**—Weave poles are 1-inch PVC pipe poles in sets of 6 to 12 poles set anywhere from 18 to 25 inches apart in a straight line. Your Lab must enter the weave poles and weave through them (hence the name).

Retriever Rewards

The height of the jumps or hurdles depends on the dog's height at the withers. Since the standard height for Labs is over 21 inches, most Labs will fall under the highest jump height in all agility classes, that being 20 to 26 inch high hurdles. A few Labs below 22 inches may qualify for the AKC 20-inch jump height.

How to Find an Agility Training Class or Club

Agility is a very popular dog sport, so if you live near a city or town, chances are there are agility clubs and trainers in your area. Contact local obedience clubs or training facilities in your area to find out where you and your Lab can train in agility. If you can't find a club or training facility, contact the national organizations or surf the web to www.dogpatch.org and check out their agility calendar. Listings for matches and trials have contact names of the trial secretary. You should be able to locate a club or facility through them.

Lab Facts

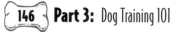

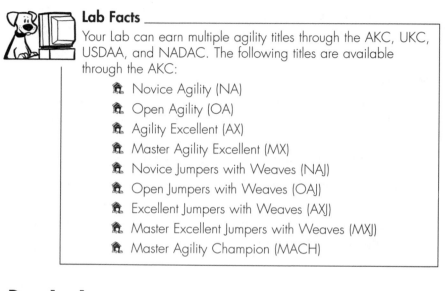

Your Lab can earn multiple agility titles through the AKC, UKC, USDAA, and NADAC. The following titles are available through the AKC:

- Novice Agility (NA)
- Open Agility (OA)
- Agility Excellent (AX)
- Master Agility Excellent (MX)
- Novice Jumpers with Weaves (NAJ)
- Open Jumpers with Weaves (OAJ)
- Excellent Jumpers with Weaves (AXJ)
- Master Excellent Jumpers with Weaves (MXJ)
- Master Agility Champion (MACH)

Retrieving

The Labrador Retriever is, of course, a hunting dog. If you're looking at training your Lab for competition or as a hunting companion, there is a whole industry designed for training hunting dogs. However, you might want to learn the basics of Retriever training.

Teaching Your Labrador Retriever to Retrieve

Training your Lab to retrieve requires breaking the act of retrieving down to its various components. First, teach your Lab to fetch. Play with a favorite toy—usually a tennis ball or a stuffed toy. After your Lab enjoys playing with it, tease him with the toy—playing a kind of keep-away. Toss the toy a short distance away when your Lab wants to grab it. Usually, he'll go after the toy at that point. Call him to you when he picks it up. Praise him and offer a treat as a trade.

If your Lab drops the toy before bringing it to you, show him the toy and tease him with it again so that he'll grab onto it. Then, offer a trade—a treat for the toy. Most Retrievers don't need a lot of training in fetch; most will play fetch readily.

(© Kent and Donna Dammen)

Two Labs who have retrieved their owners' waterfowl.

After your Lab has learned to fetch, start teaching him to retrieve with a canvas or plastic dummy designed for training bird dogs. Toss the dummy ten feet away and send your Lab to fetch it. When he returns with the dummy, praise him. If he does not fetch the dummy, walk up with him, put the dummy in his mouth, put him in stay, and walk back. Now call him. If he fails to bring the dummy, work on your Fetch command.

Lab Bites

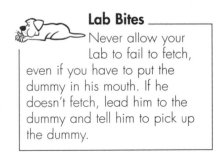

Never allow your Lab to fail to fetch, even if you have to put the dummy in his mouth. If he doesn't fetch, lead him to the dummy and tell him to pick up the dummy.

When your Lab is comfortable with fetching the dummy, increase the distance. Start at the 10-foot distance and throw the dummy in the same place. Have your Lab retrieve it. Now throw the dummy in the same place, turn around, and walk 10 feet away from your first position. Now you have 20 feet between you and the dummy. Tell your Lab to fetch. Give him lots of praise when he does fetch it.

Increase your distance, as your Lab becomes more proficient in fetching. If at any time your dog has problems with the range, decrease the distance and practice at a shorter distance.

Retriever Rewards

Most fieldwork requires that your Lab be off his leash. Don't attempt to train your Lab for hunting or retrieving work until he is reliable off his leash.

Fetching with a Thrower

Your Lab should now recognize that the dummy is a desirable thing to fetch. Now, use another person to throw the dummy. Have the thrower throw the dummy to the left or right of your Lab—not right in front of him. Now, give your Lab the command to fetch the dummy.

Keep the distances small at first and always insist that your Lab retrieves the dummy even if you must show him the dummy and help him retrieve it.

Retrieving Games

There are plenty of retrieving games you can play with your Lab. Most teach your Lab to retrieve on command. Here are a few fun ones:

- Arrange the dummies in a large diamond pattern on the ground. Clip a leash onto your Lab's collar and walk him around the dummies. As you pass by each dummy, give your Lab the command to pick it up. Praise him each time he retrieves a dummy and give him a treat.

- Arrange the dummies in a large circle. Clip a leash onto your Lab's collar and walk him around the dummies. As you pass by each dummy, give your Lab the command to pick it up. Praise him each time he retrieves a dummy and give him a treat. Toss the dummy into the center of the circle. After you've exhausted the dummies, remove the leash and take a dummy from the pile and throw it. Give your Lab the command to retrieve the dummy.
- Arrange the dummies in a large square. Choose the dummies you want your Lab to retrieve and those you don't. As you walk by, give your Lab the command to retrieve those dummies you want.

(© *Kent and Donna Dannen*)

These Labs are retrieving dummies.

Hunting Tests and Field Trials

Labrador Retrievers may participate in both Hunting Tests and Field Trials. Field Trials are extremely competitive and many have purses associated with the competition. The best way for you and your Lab to get involved in both Hunting Tests and Field Trials is to contact a local club and enter training classes.

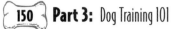

> **Lab Facts**
> A Labrador Retriever who earns his conformation championship and his field championship is a Dual Champion (DC).

The titles available in Hunting Tests are the following:

- Junior Hunter (JH)
- Senior Hunter (SH)
- Master Hunter (MH)

The titles available for Field Trials are the following:

- Field Champion (FC)
- Amateur Field Champion (AFC)

The Least You Need to Know

- Conformation showing (dog shows) is where your Lab competes against other Labs to display his conformance to the standard.
- Tracking down items and people is a sport recognized by the AKC and UKC.
- Agility is a fast-paced sport where dogs compete on an obstacle course.
- Your Lab can learn to help a hunter by retrieving birds, and he can earn titles in hunting tests and field trials.

Chapter 12

When Labs Do Good Things

In This Chapter

- What is the Canine Good Citizen title?
- Therapy Dog training
- Assistance Dog training
- Search and Rescue training

You already know how lovable Labs are. But it turns out that they are also excellent at learning to be helpful to people in a variety of different ways.

This chapter shows you how your dog can be certified as a Canine Good Citizen, which means that he behaves well around people and is neatly groomed. You'll also learn about other helpful and heroic things Labs do, such as serving as Therapy Dogs, Assistance Dogs, and Search and Rescue dogs.

Is Your Lab a Canine Good Citizen?

In 1989, the American Kennel Club created the Canine Good Citizen test to encourage responsible dog ownership. Unlike other AKC titles, the CGC title is available to all dogs, purebred or mixed breed. Although the Canine Good Citizen is not technically an official AKC title, dog owners can put CGC after their dog's name.

The Canine Good Citizen Test

The CGC is a series of tests designed to showcase a dog's good manners and appearance. The Canine Good Citizen test is pass or fail. Dogs can take and retake the CGC test until they pass. Your Lab must pass a series of ten tests to receive the CGC title:

- **Accepting a Friendly Stranger**—The dog must show no fear when a stranger approaches the dog's owner and talks to him or her.
- **Sitting Politely for Petting**—The dog must accept petting by a stranger when he is with his owner.
- **Appearance and Grooming**—The dog must accept being brushed gently by the evaluator and allow the evaluator to pick up each foot and examine the dog's ears. The dog is also judged on whether he is clean and groomed.
- **Walking on a Loose Lead**—The dog must walk on a loose lead and walk with the handler, including turns and stops.
- **Walking through a Crowd**—The dog must walk through a crowd of people without pulling, jumping on people, or acting fearful.
- **Sit and Down on Command—Staying in Place**—The dog must sit and lie down on command. The dog must then stay in place while the owner walks 20 feet away and returns to the dog. The dog may change position but must stay in the same place.

- **Coming When Called**—The dog must wait while the owner walks 10 feet and then calls him. The dog must come to the owner.
- **Reaction to Another Dog**—The dog must show no more than a casual interest in another dog as that dog and his handler approach the first dog and his owner.
- **Reaction to Distraction**—The dog must show no fear when faced with two everyday distractions. The dog may show curiosity, but not aggression or shyness.
- **Supervised Separation**—The dog must accept being left with the evaluator for three minutes while the owner is out of sight.

Training to Become a Canine Good Citizen

Training for the Canine Good Citizen requires good socialization and basic obedience. The CGC test requires that your Lab sits and lies down, and comes on command, but those are only two of the ten tests. The other tests involve good manners—that is, manners people expect from a well-behaved dog.

Some trainers teach CGC classes to prepare for the CGC test. Ideally, CGC training should start the moment you obtain your Lab as a puppy. Your Lab is ready to meet the world after he has had his last series of vaccinations—usually after 16 weeks.

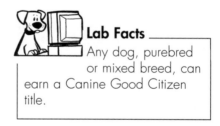

> **Lab Facts**
> Any dog, purebred or mixed breed, can earn a Canine Good Citizen title.

Bring your Lab to different places and meet different people. Going to obedience classes, fun matches, dog parks, pet-supply stores, and other places that allow dogs will help socialize your Labrador Retriever. Sometimes bringing your Lab to the mall or supermarket and having him stand outside to experience crowds may help desensitize him to strangers and crowds.

Lab Bites

If your Lab is shy—that is, he cringes when he sees other humans—you should try to bring him to places to see and meet people. Start with relatively uncrowded parks and slowly build up.

If your Lab acts very fearful or aggressive toward people, consult a professional dog behaviorist. You need to retrain and socialize him before he becomes a hazard.

Although it's unusual for a Labrador to be shy, dogs who haven't had much socialization may show fearfulness when they meet people. This is a sign that you should start bringing your Lab to different places where he has the chance to meet people.

Therapy Dogs

The Labrador Retriever's good nature makes him the perfect choice for a therapy dog. Therapy dogs provide positive support for patients in hospitals, at nursing homes, at hospices, and at other care facilities. The pet's healing effects are well known to the many volunteers who bring their dogs to these facilities. Dogs often can help withdrawn patients become less reclusive and more cooperative. Patients enjoy the dogs' nonjudgmental manner and often form special friendships with therapy dogs.

Retriever Rewards

You can get involved in a therapy dog program near you by contacting a local hospital, hospice, or nursing home. Most will be able to direct you to the person who organizes the program.

Any well-behaved Lab may become a therapy dog. Your Lab should have obedience training. He doesn't need to know tricks, but often a "Shake Hands" or "Speak" breaks the ice. Therapy dogs do not require any special training beyond good manners and general obedience training. Temperament is important and your Lab should become used to having strange people pet and touch him.

(© Kent and Donna Dannen)

Being a therapy dog can be tough, but rewarding.

Some organizations, such as Therapy Dog International and the Delta Society Pet Partners, require that your dog pass a modified version of the AKC Canine Good Citizen test. Delta Society Pet Partners requires that prospective therapy dog owners attend a workshop or complete the at-home version of the Pet Partners Team Training Course and a further aptitude test.

Assistance Dogs

Not surprisingly, Labrador Retrievers make excellent assistance dogs. Most assistance dogs are trained from the time they are eight weeks of age to become assistance dogs and come from a special breeding program. These dogs provide assistance for disabled persons, work as Seeing-Eye and hearing dogs, and are skilled companion dogs.

Lab Facts

Canine Companions for Independence is a nonprofit organization in Santa Rosa, California, that provides trained assistance dogs to people with disabilities. Founded in 1975, CCI has graduated over 1,720 human-canine teams. CCI provides service dogs, hearing dogs, skilled companion dogs, and facility dogs. CCI charges only $100 as a registration fee—everything else is paid through private contributions. CCI is one of many service organizations throughout the country.

One assistance dog program, Canine Companions for Independence, uses 40 percent Labrador Retrievers in its program. A special volunteer puppy raiser raises the puppy until he is 13 to 18 months old. Then the puppy goes into advanced training to be selected for a particular type of service work. CCI trainers pair the dogs with their prospective partners.

(Photo courtesy Canine Companions for Independence)

An assistance Lab helps his owner purchase items in a store.

CCI offers a variety of assistance dogs. These include the following:

- **Service Dogs**—These dogs assist adults who are disabled but have the physical ability to work independently with a dog.
- **Hearing Dogs**—These dogs assist people who are deaf or hard of hearing by alerting their partners to sounds.
- **Skilled Companion Dogs**—These dogs assist an adult or child with a disability and a second caretaker adult.
- **Facility Dogs**—These dogs are often called therapy dogs and work in such settings as hospitals, hospices, physical therapy programs, and programs for people with disabilities.

Retriever Rewards

Most assistance dogs are specially trained in programs like those offered in CCI. If you're interested in becoming a volunteer in CCI's puppy-raising program or wish to learn more about CCI, contact the Canine Companions for Independence, P.O. Box 446, Santa Rosa, CA 95402-0446. Phone: 707-577-1700. Website: www.caninecompanions.org.

Search and Rescue Dogs

In the aftermath of September 11, rescuers with Search and Rescue (SAR) dogs looked for missing persons at the World Trade Center and the Pentagon. Many of these SAR dogs were Labrador Retrievers, specially trained to find humans amid rubble.

SAR dog training is different than tracking in one very important way. The dogs are trained to find humans rather than the track and the items. Depending on the type of SAR work, the SAR dog may search for *any* human, alive or dead, or may search for an individual, such as a missing victim of a crime. If the SAR team can obtain an item that belonged to the victim, they use it to show the dog what scent they want him to follow.

The types of SAR dogs are as varied as the conditions:

- **Wilderness search dogs**—These dogs search for missing persons in the forest.
- **Avalanche search dogs**—These dogs search for victims buried under avalanches.
- **Disaster search dogs**—These dogs search for victims in the aftermath of disasters such as the World Trade Center tragedy, earthquakes, and tornadoes.
- **Urban search dogs**—These dogs search for victims of crimes and search for missing persons.

Lab Facts

The National Association for Search and Rescue (NASAR) certifies Search and Rescue Dogs.

The Least You Need to Know

- The Canine Good Citizen (CGC) title is open to any dog, purebred or mixed breed, and is a type of temperament test offered through the AKC.
- Therapy dogs provide comfort to patients in hospitals, hospices, nursing homes, and other care-giving facilities. Any dog may be a therapy dog provided that he has a good temperament and knows obedience.
- Assistance dogs provide a variety of tasks that aid people with disabilities. Assistance dogs are specially bred and trained when they are puppies to perform the required tasks.
- Search and Rescue dogs (SAR) are specially trained to search for victims of disasters, crime, avalanches, and so on.

Chapter 13

Recalcitrant Retrievers

In This Chapter

- How to spot a budding juvenile delinquent and correct bad behavior before it gets out of hand
- Dealing with chewing, house-soiling, jumping up, digging, escaping, and food stealing
- Stopping excessive barking
- What to do with an aggressive, anxious, or fearful dog

This chapter discusses how good Labrador Retrievers go bad and what you can do to prevent this from happening. If you're already at the stage where you're having problems, you can read about practical solutions to the most common of bad behaviors.

When Good Dogs Go Bad

Like any dog breed, Labs have their share of juvenile delinquents. One look at the local shelters will confirm that most dogs are relinquished between the ages of six months and two years. Many times, the puppy is no longer cute and has a behavior problem his owners are unwilling or unable to change.

The sad truth is that most of these dogs have behavior problems that are easily correctable with the right trainer and the right owner. But somewhere along the road, the owner decided it just wasn't worth it.

If you're reading this chapter, you're reading it for one of two reasons. The first reason is that you have a Labrador who isn't at what I call the "desperation stage"—that is, the Lab may or may not be showing signs of becoming a juvenile delinquent. The second reason: You're at the desperation stage and you've allowed the bad behavior to take a nasty turn. I've seen this before in dog-rescue work. The owner says, "I've got to fix this problem or get rid of the dog by Saturday." You've guessed it—it's Thursday night.

Lab Bites

There are no quick fixes to bad behavior. There are, however, immediate solutions that will prevent your Lab from emitting the behavior you want to change.

The bad news is, there are no quick fixes to bad behavior. Your Lab has probably had months to perfect this—a few weeks isn't going to change the behavior immediately. There is good news, though: There are immediate solutions to prevent your Lab from doing the behavior, thus giving you both a "time-out." But, you—as the owner—*must* make the changes immediately to see any type of turnaround. You must be consistent as well. You can't try the "fix" for a little while and then go back to the way you've been doing it. It doesn't work that way.

What you must do is stop the current behavior. For example, if your Lab is chewing inappropriate items, you must keep him from getting to those items. That requires crate training or watching your Lab whenever he is out of his crate. Then, you must substitute an appropriate behavior: chewing something that is appropriate.

Retriever Rewards

It is easier to teach a good behavior than to unlearn a bad behavior. If your Lab never learns the bad behavior, he won't exhibit it.

The behavior doesn't change overnight, so expect a new routine. If that means you must have your Lab in the crate while you can't watch him, then do it. But, you will also have to add exercise to his regimen to make up for the idle time.

Signs of Trouble on the Horizon

It all starts innocently enough. Your Lab growls at you when you feed him, barks and whines at the postal carrier or the neighbor's cat, or digs up a small portion of the edge of the grass. The following are signs that you may have a problem with your Lab in the future:

- He "mouths" your hands.
- He growls at you if you touch his food or toys.
- He growls at you if you tell him to move or if you push him away.
- He chews on things he shouldn't.
- He barks at people and things.
- He's able to unlatch and open doors.
- He lifts his leg in the house.

Retriever Rewards

Never allow a puppy to do something that isn't allowed as an adult. For example, Retrievers are normally very mouthy dogs and as puppies will mouth your hands. It isn't cute to have a 100-pound Retriever chewing on your hands.

What Owners Do to Encourage Bad Behavior

You may be surprised to learn that most owners encourage bad behavior. They allow puppies to get away with things "just this once." Unfortunately, Labs have long memories when it comes to doing naughty things. If you let your Lab get away with it, you've just set a precedent.

Reread the "How to Be the Alpha to Your Dog" section in Chapter 8. I've recommended these specific actions to avoid dominance problems. However, if you've glossed over it, here are some things you might be doing to encourage bad behavior:

- **Allowing your Lab to sleep in your bed.** Don't do this! You look like a littermate to your Lab and your Lab may decide to stake his claim as alpha. Have your Lab sleep in a crate beside your bed.
- **Relegating your Lab to the basement, kitchen, or wherever.** You've just shoved your Lab out of your life—the next step is out the door. Your Lab should be sleeping in a crate in your bedroom where he can bond with you.
- **Free-feeding your Labrador Retriever.** You've given him charge of his own meals, when he should be looking to you for food. Get your Lab off free feeding and feed him twice daily. It takes only a few moments to scoop out the food and set it down.
- **Giving commands and then not enforcing them.** This weakens your position.
- **Allowing your Lab up on the furniture when dominance behavior is an issue.**
- **Wrestling or playing tug-of-war games.** This puts you on an equal level to your Lab.
- **Allowing your Lab to mouth you or pull on you.**
- **Giving treats when your Lab demands it.**
- **Not exercising your Lab.** Exercising releases pent up energy.

> **Retriever Rewards**
>
> A tired Lab is a happy Lab—and one who is less likely to get into mischief. Exercising or becoming involved in an activity that both you and he will enjoy will make him less likely to have energy to challenge you or to cause mischief.

When a Behavior Appears Out of Nowhere (or Even if It Doesn't)

Surprisingly, when owners see bad behavior, the first thing they think to do is to blame the dog. Quite often, many bad behaviors have their roots in biological causes; that is, your Lab may have an underlying medical condition that may cause him to behave badly.

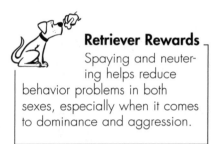

Before you attempt to make any behavioral changes, your first step is to take your Lab to your veterinarian and have a thorough physical. Tell your vet the behavior you're seeing and ask whether anything biological could cause it.

Retriever Rewards

Spaying and neutering helps reduce behavior problems in both sexes, especially when it comes to dominance and aggression.

Here is a partial list of behavior problems and possible biological causes:

- **Growling or snapping when touched**—Pain in that part of the body, abscess, tooth problems, arthritis, hip dysplasia, paneosteitis, other joint problems.
- **Growling when approaching food bowl or raiding food from the counter**—Ravenously hungry from a medical condition.
- **Aggression toward people or dogs**—Low thyroid, other hormone imbalance.
- **Marking or urinating on the floor**—Urinary tract infection, kidney problems, bladder problems.
- **Chewing inappropriate items or destructive behavior**—Tooth problems, teething.

Even if your veterinarian rules out biological problems with a certain behavior, now is the time to discuss spaying or neutering your Lab if you haven't done so yet.

Although there has been much debate on whether spaying reduces aggression in female dogs, it's been my experience that spaying and neutering helps reduce aggression and other challenging behaviors in both sexes. Female dogs who I've spayed for behavior problems have been overall less aggressive than when they were intact, suggesting a hormonal imbalance.

But spaying and neutering isn't a panacea for training. It is a tool in your training arsenal. It will help reduce unwanted behavior.

Lab Bites

Spaying and neutering is not a panacea for training. It is a tool in your training arsenal. It helps reduce unwanted behavior, but you must also work with your Lab to teach good behavior.

Destructive and Distressing Behavior

Bad behavior is often the result of allowing your Lab to get away with it, "just this once." But sometimes, even if you're vigilant, you can have a troublemaker who seems to defy the odds.

In all destructive behaviors, you need to stop them immediately. In some cases, it takes drastic action by actually preventing your Lab from doing the behavior at all and then substituting a correct behavior.

Spaying and neutering should be one of the first things you do when you're faced with an odious behavior, unless you're competing in dog shows. Even then, spaying and neutering will only help tone down the behavior—your Lab won't unlearn it through a surgery. You must work at retraining your Lab to learn a new set of behaviors.

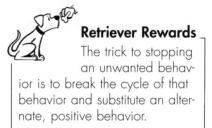

Retriever Rewards

The trick to stopping an unwanted behavior is to break the cycle of that behavior and substitute an alternate, positive behavior.

Chewing and Other Destructive Behavior

The first thing to do is analyze when your Lab is chewing on inappropriate items or being destructive. Is it when you're not home or when you're home and you can't watch your Lab? Is it a particular item your Lab is interested in, or does he choose random things?

If your Lab is a puppy and is teething, then this is normal behavior. You will have to provide acceptable chew items and crate him when you cannot watch him. If he is an older adult, have your vet look into possible teeth problems, such as puppy teeth that haven't come out or adult teeth that haven't grown properly.

> **Retriever Rewards**
>
> One trick in the trainer's repertoire is a little bonding technique I learned early on. Get a long leash (10 feet or so) and hook one end to his collar. Tie the other end to your belt or belt loop while your Lab is in the house. Now, he must follow you where you go and focus on you. When you can't watch your Lab, put him in his crate.

Once you've determined that the problem isn't biological, it's time to stop the behavior in its tracks. If your Lab isn't crate trained, or if you don't keep your Lab in a crate, start now. The crate will keep him from destroying your house. Give your Lab an appropriate chew item while you're home but unable to watch him every second.

Second, try tying your Lab to you (see the "Retriever Rewards" box). Your Lab will be unable to run off and chew up something without you seeing it. This method accomplishes two things. First, it helps prevent destructive behavior. Second, it helps bond your Lab to you. It makes your Lab focus on what you're doing instead of what he wants to do.

This bonding technique will help break the cycle in chewing, but it takes a while. When you catch your Lab chewing something inappropriate, offer an appropriate item as a trade, such as a chew item or rawhide.

House-Soiling

Your Lab should be crate trained. If he isn't or has never been properly housebroken, refer to Chapter 7.

If your Lab has started marking in the house for no apparent reason (and the reason isn't biological), start working on dominance issues (see Chapter 8) and tie your Lab to you when he is out of the crate.

If you catch him lifting his leg, correct him with a "No!" and whisk him outside. Then clean up the marking with an enzymatic cleaner.

Don't Tread on Me!—Jumping Up

Your Lab loves to jump up because he is excited or happy to see you. Instead of giving him a harsh correction, try putting him into a Sit and then crouching down to pet him. Don't pet him unless he is in a Sit position. He'll soon learn that to be petted, he must sit nicely.

If he jumps up or climbs on you, sometimes bringing up your knee so that he bounces against it with a quick Off! command works. But many dogs just bounce off and try it again. The Sit command is more effective.

Trench Warfare—Digging

Digging is a tough habit to break. You can try to break your Lab from digging by back-filling the holes with your Lab's feces and covering them with dirt, but this will only keep your Lab from digging in that spot again. You will then have to watch him to prevent further digging.

Take several pop cans and put five to ten pennies in them. Crumple them so that they hold the pennies and rattle when you shake them. When you catch your Lab digging, throw a can toward him (don't hit him!) close enough to startle him. Say, "No dig!" This should surprise him enough to stop digging.

A few pop cans and your Lab should get the idea. However, this won't work if you leave your Lab outside all day while you're gone. It is better to keep your Lab inside in a crate or in a kennel run. If you have an area in your yard that can be your Lab's kennel run, and you don't mind a hole or two, that may be a better solution than trying the pop-can method.

Some people teach their dogs to dig in one place. When they catch their dog digging in an inappropriate spot, they correct their dog and lead him to where it is okay to dig.

Retriever Rewards

Take several pop cans, put 5 to 10 pennies in them, and then crumple them. When you catch your Lab doing something bad, throw a can toward him to startle him and make him quit.

Presto-Change-o—It's Houdini!

Escape-artist dogs are made, not born, although if you're dealing with one now, you're probably convinced he has more tricks in his bag than Houdini. Most escape-artist dogs start out by being clever and bored. Combine this with ineffective barriers and you've got the makings of a Houdini.

Labs are generally not known for being Houdini dogs, but that's a small consolation if you're faced with one. Your Lab will continue to break out as long as you continue to put up ineffective barriers. The Houdini dog receives his reward from escaping. Putting up slightly better barriers simply convinces the Houdini dog that he must try harder. So he continues to escape in a sort of one-upmanship.

The trick is to have a good barrier the first time after he tries to escape. If your Lab escapes from the backyard constantly, you may have to build a special dig-proof, jump-proof, climb-proof kennel and keep your Lab inside in an escape-proof crate when you are not at home.

Prevent your Lab from becoming a Houdini by giving him something to do during those long hours. A thick marrow bone filled with peanut butter is often a fun treat for your Lab and will give him hours of tasty enjoyment. Giving him plenty of fun toys and making a small obstacle course—something to climb in and on—will help relieve some of the boredom. In the summertime, Labs enjoy a kiddie wading pool outside to splash in.

Raiding Parties

Labs are well known for raiding counters for food. If your Lab is good at raiding parties, you must remove the temptation first. Keep all food out of your Lab's reach. This may require that you install child latches on your cabinets and hide your dinner in the oven or microwave while you leave it unattended.

Most owners of garbage raiders learn to hide their trash under the kitchen sink or in the bathroom. If your Lab is particularly adept at trying to get at items on the stove, either crate him or use *static mats.* Most dogs avoid these mats after one or two jolting encounters. After that, you can leave the mat turned off or use a "dummy" mat.

Lab Lingo

Static mats—Low-shock mats that give a jolt similar to walking across a carpeted area and touching a doorknob. (Yes, I've touched one. They're unpleasant, but harmless.) These mats are far less painful than if your Lab burns himself trying to steal food off the stove.

The bad news is that once the raiding starts, it's very hard to stop it for good. After all, your Lab has received a great "reward" for stealing something. It may take months or even years to break the cycle. If you slip up and your Lab steals food (or trash) again, you're back to where you started.

Keep all food and trash away from your Lab. That means, put kiddie-proof latches on your cupboards and keep your food out of reach. It's not uncommon for me to put my food in the microwave to avoid inquisitive noses when I have to leave it unattended. Keep your trash behind a closed door or in a latched cupboard.

Barking Up the Wrong Tree—Excessive Barking

Labs who bark too much are often encouraged from the start. They see a stranger walking down the street and bark. The stranger's reaction—or perhaps your reaction if you praised him—is enough to reinforce the behavior. Soon, your Lab is "idiot barking"—that is, barking at just about anything and everything.

Idiot barkers like hearing the sound of their own voice. They're a little like people who talk too much. Unfortunately, owners of idiot barkers tend to tune out their dog's barking until the local animal control is on their doorstep with complaints from their neighbors about the barking dog.

If your Lab is barking and keeping the neighbors up at night, why are you leaving him outside? He's better off indoors in his own crate by your bed than out disturbing the neighbors. Same for the dog who sits in his outside kennel while his owners are gone to work or school.

Retriever Rewards

The spray-bottle discipline method is a little more unpleasant than the pennies in a pop can method. Fill a squirt bottle or soaker water gun with clean water. When you catch your Lab barking, squirt him. Most dogs, even water-loving Retrievers, don't like getting squirted and soon stop.

If your Lab is still noisy—indoors, while you're gone, or outside while you're home—the next step is to use the pennies in a pop can or the spray-bottle method. You can use these methods only if you are home to watch the dog.

A citronella bark collar is an alternative to a standard bark collar. When the dog barks, the collar sprays a fine mist of citronella on his chin. Most dogs dislike the smell and quickly learn to be quiet. However, some dogs are clever enough to turn their head to avoid the mist or will bark several times to empty the canister.

Standard bark collars provide an electrical stimulus or low-grade shock whenever the dog barks. These collars may be set off either by the dog's bark or the movement of the vocal cords. Most have several settings. These collars can be effective as training devices, but most owners prefer them as a last resort. If you decide to try these collars, you can't leave them on all the time or the prongs may damage your dog's neck. Use a collar that is set off by the movement of your dog's vocal cords, not the bark, or a neighbor's dog may set it off. Lastly, these collars should be used as a last resort.

Lab Facts

Getting your Lab to stop barking can be difficult. Try the following before using drastic methods such as bark collars:

- Keep your Lab inside at night and during the day when you're not at home.
- Use the pennies-in-a-pop-can method or squirt bottle method for when you are at home.
- Spend extra time with your Lab exercising and playing with him.

Personality Problems

Aggressions, anxieties, and phobias are generally more complex problems than simple destructive behavior. Dog owners whose Labs

(Photo courtesy Canine Companions for Independence)

The versatility and friendliness of the Lab make it an ideal companion as both a pet and a willing worker.

(© Jacky Sachs)

Show quality or pet quality—either type makes a great pet. This is Rosco.

(Photo courtesy Canine Companions for Independence)

Always purchase your Lab puppy from a reputable breeder.

(© Kent and Donna Dannen)

When looking for an adult Lab, look for one with a good temperament.

(© Kent and Donna Dannen)

Learn your Lab's chewing habits before allowing him to play with toys he can tear apart.

(© Kent and Donna Dannen)

This group of Labs is well behaved thanks to obedience training.

(© Kent and Donna Dannen)

Labs are exceptional in agility. This Lab is weaving through weave poles on an agility course.

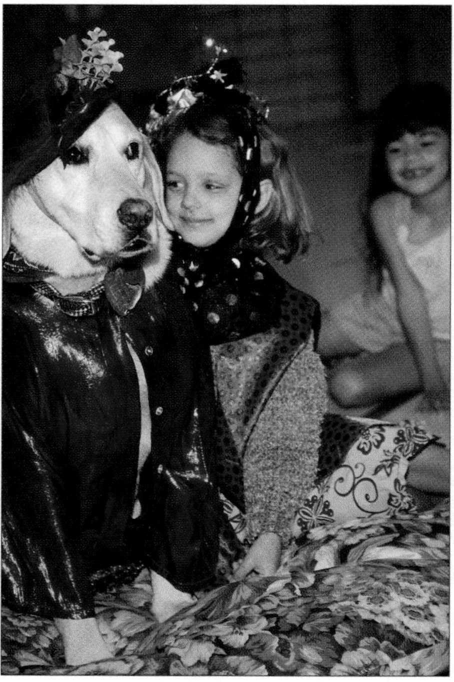

(© Kent and Donna Dannen)

Being a therapy dog can be tough, but rewarding.

(© Kent and Donna Dannen)

Your Lab puppy will benefit from a balanced diet.

(© Kent and Donna Dannen)

Four healthy Labs in the three Lab colors: Black, Chocolate, and two shades of Yellow.

(Photo courtesy Canine Companions for Independence)

Labs are skilled companion dogs.

(© Debra Su Stephens)

Exercise and preventative maintenance will help keep your Lab healthy. This is Lord Autumn's Blue Sky.

(© Debra Su Stephens)

Labs sure love to retrieve!

(© Jacky Sachs)

Puppies are adorable and Lab puppies are no exception. But be certain that you have the patience and time commitment for a puppy.

(© Jacky Sachs)

Always reward your Lab for coming to you.

(Photo courtesy Canine Companions for Independence)

These puppies are training to be service dogs.

exhibit these behaviors may have to consult behavior specialists to deal with them.

Once these behaviors start, it is difficult to eliminate them thoroughly. At the very best, you can diminish the symptoms to where it will not be a problem, but you will always have to be aware that the dog has these difficulties. For example, I've had two dogs who were afraid of thunderstorms. I know that these dogs would bolt if they were given the opportunity. Nothing that I have done has encouraged this behavior. Consequently, they are crated during thunderstorms.

Aggression

Aggression is a serious problem. If your Lab has already bitten someone or if you are afraid of him, *seek professional help immediately.* A dog like this is a liability.

There are several types of aggression, which, unfortunately, our legal system doesn't recognize:

- **Dominance aggression** occurs when the dog is trying to assert his status over another dog or a human. This may be very aggressive behavior and the dog may not back down.
- **Fear aggression** occurs when the dog feels it has been put in a dangerous situation. The dog bites out of fear to get away from the situation. It's usually a quick snap or a series of snaps followed by the dog retreating.
- **Pain aggression** is much like fear aggression, but the dog is in pain and wants the pain to stop. Again, this is usually a few quick snaps and the dog retreats.
- **Guarding** is similar to dominance aggression, but the dog is trying to keep an item away from a potential contender. Again, this is a few quick bites. The dog is unlikely to pursue the contender once the contender backs down.

- **Prey drive** is where the dog looks at the person or animal as prey and pursues it to kill it. All dogs have some form of prey drive—some being more developed than others. In a full prey drive, the dog will attack aggressively and won't stop until met with enough force to deter it.

Lab Facts

Not all aggression is bad. Humans have harnessed some aggression, such as prey drive, into useful actions. Herding, for example, is a diminished prey drive where the dog exhibits all the characteristics of a prey drive without the attack or bite at the end.

A dog may exhibit more than one type of aggression at a time. For example, a dog may show dominance aggression with guarding aggression or prey drive with dominance aggression.

It helps to understand what type of aggression you're dealing with. Different types of aggression require different action. Fear aggression, for example, requires very different handling than dominance aggression.

The key to stopping aggression is preventing it in the first place. Positive socialization will go a long way toward eliminating fear in your Lab. Neutering and spaying will help with dominance aggression. Teaching your puppy to "trade" for something tasty will help prevent guarding behavior over the food bowl.

Lab Bites

Labs are not supposed to be aggressive toward humans or animals. If your Lab shows signs of aggression, seek a professional trainer to help you train this out before it becomes a real problem.

Keeping your Lab away from aggressive dogs will help keep him from learning aggressive behavior toward other dogs. Some aggressive behavior is learned. Let's say an aggressive dog attacks your

Lab. Your Lab may be fearful that he might be attacked again the next time he sees another dog and may growl. The other dog may growl (because he's challenged), thus confirming the aggressive behavior.

Lab Bites

A few dogs are born with idiopathic (inborn) aggression. Nobody knows what causes it. In these rare cases, the dog randomly attacks without a trigger. No amount of training can stop it. Consult a veterinarian if you have a puppy who shows aggression or a dog who attacks randomly.

Don't Leave Me Alone!—Separation Anxiety

Some Labs become anxious and destructive when left alone. If your Lab destroys or chews things while you're not home or whines and cries when he's left alone, he may be suffering from separation anxiety.

You may unknowingly be causing separation anxiety in your Lab. Do you make a big production out of leaving and arriving? Do you act as though you are going and never coming back? Stop the tearful Oscar-winning performance! Make your exits and arrivals as low key as possible.

Crating your Lab will help with the overall destruction. You may have to spend a few days desensitizing your Lab to your comings and goings by taking short trips out of the house and then returning.

Retriever Rewards

If your Lab is suffering from separation anxiety, try putting on some soothing music, television, or radio with calm talk shows. You can also read a book into a tape recorder and play it back to your Lab so that he can hear your voice.

Sometimes exercising your Lab before you leave helps to tire him enough that he falls asleep before you leave.

If your Lab continues to display separation anxiety, there are medications your vet can prescribe to help him.

Fear of Thunder/Loud Noises

Some dogs suffer from fear of thunder or other loud noises. This fear seems to get worse with age and the dog doesn't "get over it."

If your Lab is terrified of thunder and lightning, keep him inside—preferably in a crate—during thunderstorms. Dogs who are afraid of thunder are likely to try to escape and may try to hurt themselves in their panic. If your Lab continues to become panicked or fearful even when crated, consider talking to your vet.

The Least You Need to Know

- Owners of delinquent dogs unwittingly encourage bad behavior.
- Many dogs go through a phase in their "teenage time" where they are very trying, but if you stay firm and consistent they will outgrow it.
- Prevent your Lab from misbehaving by crating or taking away the ability to perform the bad behavior, thereby breaking the cycle that reinforces the bad behavior.
- Substitute an acceptable behavior for the bad behavior, enforce all commands, and maintain your alpha status.
- If your Lab shows aggression toward people or severe anxiety or fear, seek professional help.

Part 4

In Sickness and in Health

Veterinary medicine has grown by leaps and bounds, even in the last 20 years. Vets know more about keeping a dog healthy and happy throughout his entire life. We know that preventative care, good nutrition, and owner education help prolong a dog's life.

Most of your Lab's health depends on you. Your vet can recommend proper nutrition and preventative medicine, but you are the one who will make the difference. You're the first one who will notice if your Lab is feeling sick. Part 4 shows you how to choose the right vet, feed your Lab properly for optimum health, and care for him when he is sick or aging.

Chapter 14

Lab Partners—Choosing a Veterinarian

- Types of veterinarians
- How to find the best dog doc for you and your Lab
- Bringing your Lab to the vet for the first time
- Vaccinations

Finding a good vet is important for your Lab's health. While there are many competent vets out there, you may have to do a little legwork to find the vet that's right for you and your Lab.

You may be surprised to learn that there are many types of vets and that not all vets offer the same services. It's up to you to determine what you're looking for in a vet. In this chapter, I discuss veterinarians, the types of practices and services they offer, and how to find a good veterinarian. I'll tell you a little about what to expect when you bring your Lab into the vet's office the first time.

I'll also discuss vaccinations—how they work, why there is now some controversy over vaccinations, and the latest developments in vaccine technology.

Dog Doctors

Next to you, the veterinarian is your Lab's best friend. Your vet is there to offer guidance in keeping your Lab healthy, but ultimately, you are responsible for your Lab's health. When you look for a vet, he or she should be compatible with you. This may sound strange, but whether or not you get along with your vet will affect whether you're willing to follow his or her directions.

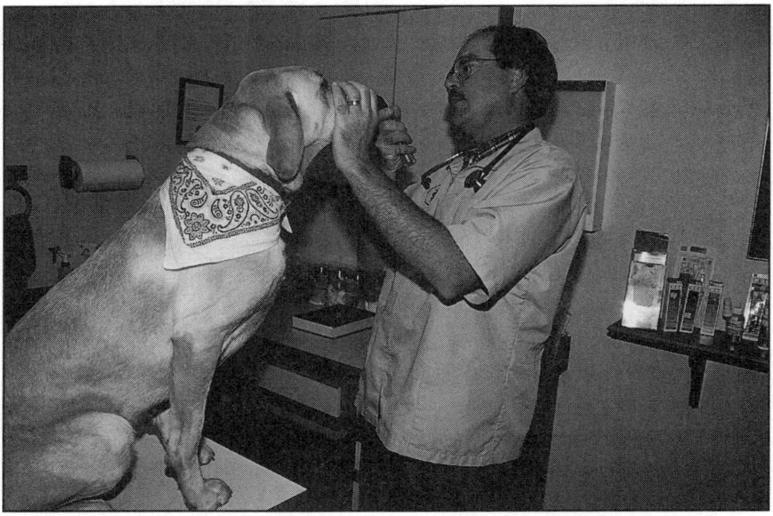

(© Kent and Donna Dannen)

The vet is important to your Lab's overall health.

Not surprisingly, there are a multitude of dog doctors around. You may see one in the local strip mall next to the dry cleaners and fast-food place. But are these vets any good? And do they have the kind of care that you're looking for?

Well, it depends. Nowadays, vets offer a variety of services, anywhere from emergency clinics, to specialists, to grooming! Some vets offer mobile clinics and true house calls, while others offer fast, convenient service and low prices. When looking for a vet, consider what you're looking for. Price shouldn't be the only consideration.

Lab Facts

Veterinarians work at various facilities. These include the following:

- **Animal hospitals**—These hospitals usually employ a large number of vets and may have specialists. These facilities may have their own testing facilities that a smaller clinic can't afford. They may handle complex surgeries and emergencies that can't be treated anywhere else.
- **Veterinary clinics**—Vet clinics may have as few as one or as many as five or more vets. These clinics have office hours and may or may not handle emergencies.
- **Emergency clinics**—These vet clinics are for emergencies only. They usually handle after-hours calls and tend to be expensive.
- **Low-cost clinics**—A relatively new type of vet clinic, the purpose behind most low-cost clinics is to provide routine services (such as vaccinations, heartworm tests, and spay/neuters) at a low cost. These clinics make up for the lower price in volume. They generally don't have the facilities to handle emergencies or complex diagnoses.
- **Mobile clinics**—Usually a limited clinic, these mobile clinics are generally associated with an animal hospital or a veterinary clinic. These offer convenience to the pet owner.

Lab Search—Finding the Best Dog Doc for Your Lab

So, how do you find the right vet for your Lab? It's quite simple: Ask your dog-owning friends who they take their dogs to. The good vets don't need to advertise—usually all it takes is word-of-mouth.

If your friends don't give their vets glowing recommendations, perhaps you need to ask your Lab's breeder or ask a local trainer.

Even if your breeder doesn't live in your area, she might be able to ask local Lab breeders who they use for veterinarians. If that doesn't work, consider contacting the American Animal Hospital Association (www.aahanet.org) or the American Veterinary Medical Association (www.avma.org) for a list of vets in your area (see Appendix B for contact information).

Retriever Rewards

If you're on a budget, perhaps a low-cost clinic might work for you. These clinics offer low prices on routine care, such as spays and neuters, vaccinations, and heartworm tests. But these clinics are seldom full-service facilities and are unable to handle emergencies or more complex procedures.

Questions to Ask

When you have a list of vets, call them and ask questions. The following questions will help narrow down your choices. There are no right or wrong answers to these questions. Some may be more important to you than others.

- What is the cost for vaccinations, office visits, and other routine services?
- What hours is your clinic open? Do you offer after-hours services?
- Do you handle emergencies or are you affiliated with a clinic that handles emergencies? Are the vets on-call and do they have on-call pagers?
- Do any of the vets specialize in a particular area such as allergies, neurology, or holistic treatments?
- Do you offer an on-site groomer or boarding?
- Do you offer a multi-pet discount?
- Do you take pet insurance?

- Do you make house calls? Under what circumstances?
- How many Labrador Retrievers does the vet see?

The staff at the clinic should be courteous and willing to answer your questions.

Lab Facts

Most pet health insurance plans don't cover costs for routine care, such as vaccinations, but handle catastrophic illnesses and injuries. They don't cover preexisting conditions and often have a deductible. As an alternative to pet health insurance, some clinics and vets offer a form of veterinary savings plan.

Vet Visitations

Once you've narrowed down the vets to a few choices, call up the vets and schedule an appointment to visit their facilities. Don't drop by unannounced—you may show up during a busy time when the staff may not have a chance to talk with you. When you do visit, ask for a tour. The clinic should be clean and the staff should be friendly and helpful. If you have a chance to talk with the vet, do so. Find out what the vet's training is and if he is familiar with conditions common to Labs. If you're interested in alternative medicine, find out if the veterinarian uses alternative therapies or is strictly a conventional vet.

You should have a good feeling about the veterinarian and the clinic before bringing your Lab there. Usually the final test is when you bring your Lab for his first appointment. While some dogs won't get along with any vet, the vet should have a gentle and caring manner toward your Lab.

Meet the Vet—Your Lab's First Visit

Your first stop before bringing your Lab home should be to the veterinarian. Most breeders require that you bring your puppy to a vet for a thorough checkup within the first week. This ensures that the puppy is in good condition when he leaves the breeder's home.

Your veterinarian should give your puppy a thorough exam. He should listen to your Lab's heart and check him over for any problems. Most vets will ask what you are feeding your puppy and make recommendations. Your vet will most likely discuss proper puppy health care and the benefits of spaying or neutering.

Retriever Rewards

When you go to the vet for the first time, bring your Lab's health records with you—if the breeder provided any. Call beforehand to ask whether the vet would like a fecal sample. If the answer is yes, bring the sample in a plastic baggie.

Now is the time to ask any questions concerning your Lab's health. Don't feel silly asking questions—most vets have heard it all before. If you don't understand something your vet says, ask! Most vet clinics also have excellent handouts on medical issues and training.

Your vet will also discuss vaccinations with you. Depending on your vet's philosophy concerning vaccinations, you may be vaccinating your puppy at this time.

Vaccinations

Vaccinations will help immunize your Lab against deadly diseases such as rabies, distemper, and parvovirus. Your Lab can actually transmit some of these diseases, such as rabies and leptospirosis, to you. Others (such as rabies and distemper) have a very high mortality rate—up to 100%. Follow your vet's advice concerning vaccines.

Vaccination Explanation

Puppies receive antibodies through their mother's colostrum—milk produced during the 24 hours after the puppies are born. These maternal antibodies protect the puppy for several weeks. Sometime after the fifth week, these antibodies fade, leaving the puppy vulnerable to disease.

Vets usually vaccinate puppies several times. It does no good to vaccinate a puppy before the maternal antibodies fade because the antibodies will override the body's immune response. Unfortunately, we don't know when these antibodies go away—they vary from puppy to puppy—so vets try to vaccinate the puppy after the maternal antibodies go away and before the puppy becomes exposed to diseases.

Lab Facts

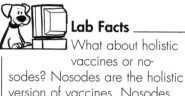

What about holistic vaccines or nosodes? Nosodes are the holistic version of vaccines. Nosodes are not FDA approved for preventing any disease and there is no scientific evidence to show that nosodes work.

Breakthroughs in Vaccination Technology

Lately, there have been some new developments in vaccines. Originally, there were only two types of vaccines, modified live vaccines and killed vaccines. In modified live vaccines, the disease is changed enough so that it appears and replicates just like the disease but won't cause the illness. This is done by introducing the disease into an unusual host, aging the disease, or modifying it in a tissue culture. In killed vaccines, the actual disease is used and then killed so that it can't reproduce.

Lab Facts

If you think recombinant vaccines are cool, just wait! Scientists are working to produce vaccines where just the DNA or RNA molecules or just the protein of the disease is used. These vaccines will have virtually no dangerous side effects or allergic reactions. Vets will have to use a special "DNA gun" to inject the DNA or RNA into the dog.

New vaccines, called recombinant vaccines, provide an even greater effectiveness, thanks to latest genetic research. There are two type of recombinant vaccines: genetic deleted recombinant and live agent recombinant vector. In genetic deleted recombinant vaccines, the organisms are modified by selectively removing genetic code for virulence factors, thus making the disease harmless. In live agent recombinant, the genetic code of the disease is inserted into a "carrier" that passes the disease's genetic code on. Both types of vaccines appear to be more effective than the modified live or killed vaccines.

Holistic Thoughts—Vaccination Controversies

The current thinking is that vaccines produce an immune response each time a vet administers a vaccine. The question is, are we overstressing our dogs' immune systems and causing autoimmune disorders?

Most holistic vets think we are and recommend that we don't vaccinate or change our current vaccination schedules. Many point out that dogs may keep their immunity to the disease for several years—not just for a year as previously thought.

Lab Bites

Although allergic reactions to vaccines are uncommon, you should always watch your Lab for a reaction. The most common reaction is swelling and puffiness in the face. A rare reaction is anaphylactic shock, where your Lab has difficulty breathing and becomes shocky (pale gums, rapid breathing, in distress). If your Lab shows any of these symptoms, obtain veterinary assistance immediately.

This is certainly a tough call. Vaccination schedules are currently under review by experts. I tend to be conservative when it comes to vaccinations and opt to vaccinate every year. A number of vets would agree with me. Still, Colorado State University, among other veterinary schools, recommends vaccinations every three years.

What Vaccinations Does My Dog Need?

As vaccination technology becomes more sophisticated, we may see more vaccines against different diseases. Recently, vaccine manufacturers have introduced Lyme and giardia vaccines.

Does your Lab need to be immunized against everything? Not necessarily. You should definitely vaccinate your Lab against diseases such as rabies, parvovirus, and distemper, but the amount of exposure should dictate whether you need to vaccinate your Lab against kennel cough, leptospirosis, giardia, and Lyme disease. Talk with your veterinarian about these vaccines and whether your Lab is at high risk for these diseases.

Lab Bites

Is your Lab at high risk to contract certain diseases? It depends. If you show your Lab, enter him in field trials, board him, or otherwise expose him to a large number of dogs, then yes, your Lab is at greater risk for contracting certain types of diseases. Likewise, if you do a lot of outdoor training in certain areas, your Lab may be at risk for contracting giardia and Lyme disease.

The best thing to do is talk with your vet. He or she can recommend a vaccination regimen that will best protect your pet.

There are many vaccines out there; however, not all vaccines may be appropriate for your Lab. Your vet can recommend the right combination of vaccines to protect your dog. Your veterinarian has vaccines that will protect against the following diseases:

- **Rabies**—This disease is caused by a virus and is nearly 100 percent fatal. There are two types of rabies: dumb (paralytic) and furious. Both types affect the central nervous system. In dumb rabies, the dog's throat becomes paralyzed, causing excessive salivation (drooling) and inability to swallow. Furious rabies is the classic "mad dog" form, where the dog becomes vicious and attacks anything. Furious rabies eventually progresses to the paralytic stage. Death follows within a few days.

Rabies is contagious to humans and is transmitted through the dog's saliva—either through a bite or through wounds in the skin. The incubation period varies considerably: anywhere from three weeks to three months or more.

- **Canine Distemper (CDV)**—This disease is almost always fatal. Distemper starts with a yellow-gray discharge from nose and eyes, high temperature, dry cough, and lethargy. It may progress to appetite loss, diarrhea, and vomiting. Distemper may affect the intestinal tract or may attack the nervous system, causing seizures and convulsions. Some dogs may have hardening of the pads, hence the name "hardpad disease." Distemper is highly contagious among dogs and may be transmitted through the air, on shoes, or on clothing. Its incubation period is about three to six days.
- **Canine Adenovirus (CA_2)**—Canine Adenovirus-2 is a form of kennel cough. Dogs who contract kennel cough have a harsh, dry cough and may sound like they are gagging. Unless the dog is very old or young, kennel cough is more of a nuisance than a danger. It is highly infectious and is transmitted through the air. The incubation period is between 5 and 10 days.
- **Infectious Canine Hepatitis (CA_1)**—Infectious Canine Hepatitis is a form of adenovirus that causes fever, lethargy, jaundice (due to liver involvement), excessive thirst, vomiting, eye and nasal discharge, bloody diarrhea, hunched back, hemorrhage, and conjunctivitis. Infectious Canine Hepatitis may attack the kidneys, liver, eyes, and the lining of blood vessels. Both CA_1 and distemper may occur simultaneously. It's contagious through an infected dog's

Lab Facts

Canine Infectious Tracheobronchitis, or "Kennel Cough," is actually caused by a number of viruses and bacteria, including Bordetella bronchiseptica, canine parainfluenza, and canine adenovirus-2.

urine, feces, and saliva. Its incubation period is between four and nine days. It is much less common.

- **Canine Parainfluenza**—Canine Parainfluenza is another form of kennel cough. Dogs who contract kennel cough have a harsh, dry cough and may sound like they are gagging. Unless the dog is very old or young, kennel cough is more of a nuisance than a danger. It is highly infectious and is transmitted through the air. The incubation period is between 5 and 10 days.
- **Leptospirosis**—This bacteria infection's symptoms include high fever, frequent urination, brown substance on tongue, lack of appetite, renal failure, hunched back, bloody vomit and diarrhea, mild conjunctivitis, and depression. It is contagious to humans. Dogs may contract leptospirosis from rats, infected water supplies, and other infected dogs. The incubation period is between 5 and 15 days. The old strains of leptospirosis were seldom fatal, with only a 10 percent mortality rate, but new strains are more deadly.
- **Canine Parvovirus**—This nasty virus appeared in 1978. It's characterized by severe, bloody diarrhea, vomiting, dehydration, high fever, and depression. "Parvo" is highly infectious and is transmitted through fecal matter. The virus can live up to one year in the soil and can be carried on shoes or paws. It has a 7 to 10 day incubation period and a 50 percent mortality rate.
- **Canine Coronavirus**—A less deadly virus than parvovirus, coronavirus looks a lot like a milder form of parvovirus. Indeed, both parvovirus and coronavirus may infect a dog simultaneously. Coronavirus is transmitted through fecal matter. It has a 24 to 36 hour incubation period.

Lab Facts

Vaccine manufacturers have approved most vaccines for yearly administration. Only certain rabies vaccines are approved for administration once every three years.

- **Bordetella bronchiseptica**—Bordetella bronchiseptica is a form of kennel cough. Dogs who contract kennel cough have a harsh, dry cough and may sound like they are gagging. Unless the dog is very old or young, kennel cough is more of a nuisance than a danger. It is highly infectious and is transmitted through the air. The incubation period is between 5 and 10 days.
- **Lyme (Borellosis)**—Lyme disease is a tick-borne disease that appeared in Lyme, Connecticut in 1975. Lyme is fairly common along the East Coast and Upper Midwest in the United States, and continues to spread. Lyme's symptoms can make the disease difficult to diagnose: fever, lameness, loss of appetite, and fatigue. Lyme is transmitted through deer ticks. The primary hosts are deer and mice.
- **Giardia**—Giardia is a microscopic organism that lives in streams. Carried by beavers and other wildlife, as well as domesticated animals, giardia was confined to the Rocky Mountains, but may be found in any untreated water. Giardia causes severe diarrhea, vomiting, and weight loss.

The Least You Need to Know

- Ask your dog-owning friends whom they would recommend for a veterinarian. The best way to find a good veterinarian in your area is word of mouth.
- When looking for a vet, find out what office hours he has, whether he has provisions for emergency service, how much he charges for routine services, and what type of services are available. It's also important to find a vet that you trust.
- Use your Lab's first visit to ask any questions you might have concerning your Lab's health, nutrition, or even training.
- Vaccines are important and will help protect your Lab against deadly diseases. Follow your veterinarian's recommendations concerning your Lab's health and vaccination schedule.

Chapter 15

Inside and Out: The Battle of the Bugs

In This Chapter

- Roundworms, hookworms, tapeworms, whipworms, and heartworms
- Dangerous bugs on the outside: fleas, ticks, and mites

Internal and external parasites can make your Lab miserable. Worse than that, they can seriously affect your Lab's health.

In this chapter, you'll learn about both internal and external parasites. You'll learn how to recognize signs of infestation and what the best course of treatment is.

I'll also discuss potential diseases transmitted from these nasty critters. Some of them, such as Lyme, can be transmitted to you if you aren't careful.

Worms

You always hear about dogs having worms, but there are actually many different types—all nasty. The following sections help you tell the difference between roundworms, hookworms, tapeworms, whipworms, and heartworm.

Roundworms

Roundworms (*Toxocara canis*) are the most common worms. Puppies frequently contract roundworms from their mothers. If your Lab's mother has ever had roundworms during her life, your puppy has probably contracted them. Contracting roundworms is not a statement about the breeder's care. However, the breeder should deworm the puppies. Roundworms lie dormant in a female dog's body and start migrating to the puppies when the female becomes pregnant. The female can further infect her puppies through her milk. Other avenues for transmission include fecal matter.

Roundworm infestation can be serious in puppies and in old and debilitated dogs. If your Lab has roundworms, this means that roundworms are benefiting from food intended for your Lab.

Lab Bites

Don't use over-the-counter dewormers on your Lab. Many of these dewormers are poisonous if used incorrectly and don't work on all forms of worms. Instead, bring a fecal sample to your vet. He can properly diagnose the type of worms and prescribe the right medication.

If he is infested with roundworms, your Lab may have a potbelly, may lose weight, and may have a poor haircoat. Other signs include vomiting, diarrhea, and a garlic odor to the breath. Take your puppy and a fecal sample to the vet. Roundworms can be quite serious and can kill a puppy. Roundworms can also be passed to people (especially children) by ingesting roundworm eggs through contact with infected feces.

Hookworms

Hookworms (*Ancylostoma caninum*) are smaller than roundworms and feed off your Lab's blood in the small intestine. These worms infest your Lab by penetrating the skin or through the mother's milk.

Severe infestations can be life threatening and can cause severe anemia. Diarrhea, weight loss, and lethargy are also signs of hookworm infestation.

Tapeworms

Tapeworms (*Dipylidium caninum*) are long, flat worms that may infest your Lab's intestines. These worms may break off and be excreted in your Lab's feces. They look like grains of rice in the feces or around the dog's anus.

Fleas commonly carry tapeworms. Your Lab may swallow a flea, thus becoming infested with tapeworms. Other modes of transmission include raw game meat. Some dogs catch and eat mice or other rodents, which carry tapeworms.

Whipworms

Whipworms (*Trichuris vulpis*) are difficult to diagnose because they don't always produce eggs in fecal matter. These worms feed on blood in the large intestine. Like hookworms, these worms can be serious and cause severe anemia. Dogs become infested by eating something in contaminated soil.

Heartworm

Heartworm is an internal parasite that can kill your Labrador Retriever. Most states within the continental United States have heartworm, although it is less prevalent in the Western states.

Mosquitoes transmit heartworm by feeding on an infected dog. The *microfilariae* or heartworm larvae from the infected dog incubate within the mosquito for several days. When the infected

Lab Lingo

Microfilariae—Heartworm larvae that infect a dog.

mosquito feeds off another dog, it injects the infectious microfilariae into the dog and the dog becomes infected with heartworm. Heartworm, when left untreated, will cause debilitation, cardiac failure, respiratory problems, and eventually death.

Regardless of where you live, you should have your Lab tested for heartworm once a year and put on a heartworm preventative. In many areas, heartworm is seasonal and you have to administer the preventative only during the spring and summer months. Heartworm season is year-round in the Southern states and areas where the temperatures seldom reach freezing.

> **Retriever Rewards**
>
> It is less expensive and risky to prevent heartworms than it is to treat them. Areas with cold climates require six months of heartworm preventative. Warmer areas require that the dog must be on heartworm preventative year-round.

Your veterinarian should administer a heartworm test before putting your Lab on preventative medication. It is a simple blood test that screens for the presence of microfilariae.

Preventatives

Several different heartworm preventatives are available, including some that actually help control other worms. Most veterinarians now prescribe monthly heartworm preventatives, although there are still a few daily preventatives available. Do not use the daily preventatives; they are less effective than the monthly preventatives if administered incorrectly.

There are several types of heartworm preventative. These include the following:

- **Heartgard (Ivermectin)**—This is the oldest form of monthly heartworm preventative. Heartgard Plus can also control roundworms and hookworms. Some dogs are sensitive to Ivermectin, but this sensitivity is rare.

- **Interceptor (Milbemycin) and Sentinel (Milbemycin and Lufenuron)**—Interceptor controls heartworm as well as hookworms, roundworms, and whipworms in a monthly preventative. Sentinel also controls fleas.
- **Revolution (Selamectin)**—A topical application, Revolution works as a monthly heartworm and flea preventative.
- **Proheart 6 (Moxidectin)**—A six-month preventative, Proheart 6 is given as an injection and can be administered only by your vet.

Treatment for Heartworm

If your Lab is heartworm positive, your veterinarian will have to treat him for heartworms. Heartworm treatment is still risky, but is now safer and less painful than the old treatment. The new treatment requires two injections. If your Lab has heartworms, be certain that your veterinarian is using a treatment newer than the old arsenic-based solution.

External Parasites

The external parasites are as bad as the internal parasites at making your dog miserable and affecting his health. More than just a nuisance, fleas and ticks harbor dangerous diseases.

Fleas

Fleas thrive in all climates except the very cold, the very dry, and high altitudes. If you live in one of these climates, you're feeling very smug right now. If you don't, you're probably looking at a map to find such a place. Fleas are horrible critters and are hard to get rid of once you have them.

If you suspect a flea infestation, search for fleas on your Lab around his belly and groin area, at the base of his tail, and around his ears. A common sign of fleas are deposits of black flea feces that turn red when wet.

If you find fleas on your Lab, you can guarantee that you have a flea infestation in your home. Talk to your veterinarian about ways to combat the problem. Often, your veterinarian can recommend a system that will combat fleas in the yard, in your house, and on your dog.

Lab Bites

Fleas are more than just annoying hard-shelled insects that feed on blood and make your Lab miserable. Fleas are carriers of tapeworm and bubonic plague, which can severely affect your Lab's health. Bubonic plague is deadly and you can contract it as well as your Lab. Fleas carry other diseases, too, so don't consider them just a nuisance.

Declaring War on Fleas

Once you find fleas, the best thing to do is contact your vet for recommendations. Your vet will recommend products based on your climate and your Lab's age and health. He will also recommend products that are safe to use together. Be very careful about mixing products and always read the labels. Systemic treatments have made most drastic measures obsolete except in the worst infestations.

If your Lab has fleas, remember that all your pets need to be treated, even if they stay indoors. Don't use dog products on your cat, rabbit, ferret, mice, and so on. Instead, use a product that is made especially for them or contact your vet for advice.

Retriever Rewards

Slip a piece of flea-control collar into the vacuum-cleaner bag to help kill the fleas it holds. Then, throw away the vacuum cleaner bag in a Dumpster—you don't need the fleas to find their way back out into your house.

You'll also have to vacuum all carpets and furniture—anywhere fleas hide. I've heard of putting a piece of flea collar in the vacuum cleaner bag to kill the fleas so that they can't get out and reinfest your home.

Your Latest Arsenal

The old flea and tick products worked by poisoning. Unfortunately, that poison could also affect your dog or you. Nowadays, the systemic treatments work on the insects by preventing the fleas from laying fertile eggs or preventing the insects from developing into adults. Some of these products prevent ticks.

Some of these systemic treatments are the following:

- **Frontline (Fipronil)** and **Frontline Plus (Fipronil and Methoprene)** works by killing fleas within 24 to 48 hours. Frontline Plus contains an insect growth regulator that keeps immature fleas from reproducing. It is a topical, spot-on systemic (in other words, you put it on the dog) that works for three months on adult fleas and one month on ticks.
- **Advantage (Imidacloprid)** works by killing both adult fleas and larvae within 48 hours. It is a topical, spot-on systemic that works for six weeks on adult fleas.
- **Program (Lufenuron)** works by preventing flea eggs from hatching or maturing into adults. It is a pill you give once a month.
- **Biospot (pyrethrins and fenoxycarb)** is a topical spot-on systemic that kills fleas and ticks for one month. It has an insect growth regulator that keeps immature fleas from reproducing. I've also seen it repel flies.

Over-the-Counter Weapons

Be extremely careful when working with insecticides. These are poisons and can harm your dog if used improperly. Some medications and wormers may react with certain pesticides, so it is very

Lab Bites

You may be surprised to learn that flea collars on your dog are usually ineffective against fleas. They can also be poisonous, especially if your Lab chews and swallows them.

important to be certain that what you are using will not interact with other pesticides or medications. Contact your veterinarian or your local poison-control center concerning their safety.

When you do select a system, find one that will work together in your home, in your yard, and on your dog. Many manufacturers make flea-control products that are intended to work together as a complete solution.

Ticks

Ticks are nasty relatives of the spider. Ticks carry dangerous diseases such as Rocky Mountain Spotted Fever, Lyme disease, and Ehrlichiosis. If your Lab has been outside for any period of time or has run through deep underbrush, you should check him over for ticks.

How to Remove a Tick

If you find a tick on your Lab, avoid handling it or you may risk exposing yourself to these diseases. Instead, follow these steps:

1. Treat the area with a good tick insecticide approved for use on dogs.
2. Wait a few minutes.
3. Try to remove it. Wear latex gloves and use tweezers. Firmly grasp the tick with the tweezers and gently pull. Don't try to pull the tick out if it resists. You may leave portions of it embedded in your dog, which may become infected.
4. If you were unable to pull out the tick, wait for it to drop off and then dispose of it.

Retriever Rewards

One vet I know recommends Preventic tick collars to prevent ticks from attaching to dogs. They are very effective against ticks, but not against fleas. As with any collar, it can be poisonous if your Lab chews and swallows it.

Tick-Borne Diseases

Ticks carry a variety of diseases including Lyme Disease, Canine Ehrlichiosis, Babesiosis, and Rocky Mountain Spotted Fever.

- **Lyme disease**—Common signs of Lyme disease are lameness and fever. A dog with Lyme disease may lack appetite, be unusually tired, and may have swelling of the lymph nodes. The dog may have bouts of unexplained lameness that may become chronic.
- **Canine Ehrlichiosis**—Common signs of Canine Ehrlichiosis are fever, discharge from the eyes and nose, and swollen limbs (edema). A dog with Canine Ehrlichiosis may lack appetite, be unusually tired, and may have swelling of the lymph nodes.
- **Babesiosis**—Common signs of Babesiosis are fever, lethargy, and lack of appetite.
- **Rocky Mountain Spotted Fever**—Common signs of RMSF are high fever, abdominal pain, coughing, lack of appetite, lethargy, swelling of face or limbs, depression, vomiting, diarrhea, and muscle or joint pain.

These diseases can greatly affect your Lab's health or may even be fatal in extreme cases. Your vet can test for tick diseases through a blood test and can treat them with medications.

If your Lab tests positive for one of these tick-borne diseases, you may wish to consider having your own doctor test you for the same diseases. Ticks can transmit these diseases to humans. In rare instances, contact with your dog's bodily fluids may transmit these diseases to you. Dispose of a tick by sealing it in a jar with bleach or flushing it down the toilet. Don't squish it between your fingers or simply dump it in the trash.

Mites

Mites are microscopic arachnids, related to ticks and spiders. There are several types of mites, including those that cause sarcoptic and demodectic mange and those that enter the ears and cause infection. Your vet can diagnose your Lab with skin scrapings to determine whether he has mites and what type they are.

Ear Mites

Ear mites (*Otodectes cynotis*) will make your Lab miserable. If your Lab has reddish-brown earwax, he may have ear mites, especially if he scratches or shakes his head frequently.

Lab Bites

A Lab's floppy ears are prone to harboring mites and bacterial infections, so it is very important to keep your dog's ears clean.

Don't try to treat ear mites with over-the-counter solutions because there may already be a secondary infection. Your vet will need to clean out the reddish-brown gunk and then will give you ear drops to kill the mites and handle any infections.

Mange Mites

There are two types of mites that cause mange. Demodectic (*Demodex canis*) mites feed primarily on the cells of the hair follicle. The infestation appears as dry, scaly red skin, with hair loss, mostly around the face. Demodectic mange exists on all dogs, but is thought to be triggered by a depressed immune system. Most of the time, localized demodectic mange clears up on its own. If it is generalized or doesn't clear up, it is hard to treat.

Sarcoptic mites (*Sarcoptes scabei*) are highly contagious. This mange may spread quickly in kennels. It is itchy and causes hair loss and a red rash. The dog may have ugly sores from scratching. Your vet can prescribe a topical product to treat sarcoptic mange. You may have to treat your Lab with medicated baths and body dips. If the sores are infected, your vet may prescribe antibiotics.

The Least You Need to Know

- Internal parasites such as the various types of worms can severely affect the health of your Lab, as well as you and your family. You should not treat them as normal or commonplace, and you should not use over-the-counter dewormers.
- Fleas and ticks carry and spread diseases, some of them deadly to dogs and humans.
- There are several types of mites, including ear mites and mange mites. Contact your vet for appropriate diagnosis and treatment.

Chapter 16

Food for Thought: Nutrition

In This Chapter

- Learn what good nutrition is for your Lab and how to select the right food
- Should you cook for your Lab?
- Special diets for canine atheletes and overweight dogs
- Foods to avoid at all costs

Garbage in, garbage out. That saying could be talking about dog nutrition. Without good, available proteins, fats, and carbohydrates, your Lab won't be at his optimal health. You may be surprised that not all dog foods are the same.

In this chapter, you'll learn about dog foods and what meat by-products really are. You'll learn how to spot a good premium brand of dog food and what will work best for your Lab, depending on his age and activity level.

You'll also learn about fad diets and home-cooked diets. Are these as good as the proponents say? Lastly, we'll talk about pudgy pooches and the necessity to keep your Lab trim.

Balancing Act—Choosing the Right Dog Food

Dog foods aren't what they used to be. Thank goodness! Dog food manufacturers have come a long way with dog food nutrition. Many are doing research with canine athletes to discover what's best for the active dog.

These companies produce some of the most scientifically formulated dog foods to keep your Lab healthy. Most are formulated to meet or exceed AAFCO (American Association of Feed Control Officials) guidelines and are tested in field trials. Dog food manufacturers are now concerned with digestibility as well as palatability.

When you select a dog food, look for a premium dog food from a recognizable company. It needs to be premium because there is less waste or filler. It needs to be recognizable because you want to be able to find it at the local pet-supply store if Hoity-Toity Pet Boutique runs out. Premium pet foods tend to have more digestible protein, meaning that your Lab can use it. The more digestible a dog food is, the less waste you will have to scoop up in your yard.

Not all dog foods are the same. Cheaper, so-called "bargain brands" may have the same nutritional analysis, but they are very different in terms of quality of ingredients. Certain ingredients may have the same protein but aren't usable by the dog.

Pick a dog food and stick with it. Don't change dog foods frequently or your Lab will become picky and may decide that none of them are to his liking.

Retriever Rewards

Your veterinarian can recommend dog food for certain medical conditions such as kidney problems or obesity.

Retriever Rewards

If you must switch dog foods, do so gradually to minimize stomach upset. Start with 10 percent of the new dog food and 90 percent of the old dog food the first day; 20 percent new and 80 percent old the second day; 30 percent new and 70 percent old the third day; and so on.

Canned, Dry, Frozen, or Semi-Moist?

Before you choose a brand of food, you need to decide what type of food you intend to feed. The most common types are dry, canned, semi-moist, and frozen.

- **Dry dog food**—Pound for pound, dry dog food or *kibble* is the most cost-effective dog food. You also have more choices in dry dog food.
- **Canned dog food**—Canned dog food is very palatable but can be expensive because you pay for the water and processing that goes into it. Many Lab owners like to add a can to their dog's dry food as a treat.
- **Semi-moist food**—Semi-moist food is chock-full of colors, preservatives, and sugar. Expensive. Use sparingly or as treats.
- **Frozen food**—Usually frozen food has no preservatives, and so it must be kept frozen to avoid bacterial growth or spoilage. Expensive—you're paying for both water weight and freezer storage.

Lab Bites

Should your Lab be a vegetarian? The answer is no. Most vegetarian diets are based on soy protein. Soy can cause gas and bloating in dogs who are allergic to it. While dogs can and do subsist on vegetarian diets, dogs are made to eat meat, not grains. If you want to be a vegetarian, that's fine. But feed your dog meat-based dog food.

Choosing a Dry Food with the Right Nutrients

Use these guidelines in selecting a dry dog food for your Lab:

- If your Lab is under 12 months old, you should still be feeding a premium puppy food. Most puppy foods have 28 percent protein and 17 percent fat by weight content, or more.

- If your Lab is an active adult, you should feed him a premium active adult food that has approximately a 25 percent protein and 15 percent fat by weight content.
- If your Lab is overweight or inactive, you should feed him a maintenance or "lite" version of the premium adult food.
- If your Lab works (in field trials or other hard work), feed him a premium performance dog food that has approximately 30 percent protein and 15 percent fat by weight content.
- If your Lab is a "senior" (over 8 years), feed him a dog food that maintains his weight and energy level. Don't switch him to a senior type dog food unless he is gaining weight or has some underlying health problem.

Retriever Rewards

Follow the guidelines on the dog food's label for feeding and adjust the amount accordingly. Most dog foods tend to recommend more than the dog actually needs to avoid underfeeding. Guidelines are just that—you must customize the amount to your individual dog.

Most dog food labels recommend a daily ration. If your Lab puppy is under four months, feed him the ration split into thirds three times a day. Otherwise, feed him half the ration twice a day.

The following sections give you more information about the essential nutrients in dog food: Protein, fat, and carbohydrates.

Protein

Protein is an essential nutrient. It provides 4 kilocalories of energy per gram and provides the building blocks for muscles, bones, organs, and connective tissue. It is the main component of enzymes, hormones, and antibodies. It helps to repair muscles, to build and maintain plasma volume and red blood cells, and to build mitochondrial volume in working dogs.

> **Lab Facts**
>
> No doubt you've heard that Ethoxyquin, a preservative in some dog foods, is bad for your dog. Opponents to Ethoxyquin claim it causes everything from tumors and cancer to aborted puppies. Although there is no scientific proof that Ethoxyquin is bad for your dog, most premium dog food manufacturers have changed to other preservatives such as tocopherols (Vitamin E) and other preservatives that are less effective. Dog food companies are sensitive to public image and would rather change an ingredient than fight an uphill battle.
>
> If Ethoxyquin is the preservative in your Lab's dog food, don't panic. Remember, there is no scientific proof that Ethoxyquin is bad.

The type of protein your dog gets is very important. Dogs are carnivores and require complete proteins that are difficult to get from vegetable sources. Good sources of protein include meat (including chicken and poultry), meat meal, meat by-products, and meat by-product meals. Although we humans think that chowing down on lungs, hearts, and intestines is gross, our dogs love them and they're actually good sources of protein.

> **Lab Facts**
>
> Don't turn up your nose at feeding your pet a dog food with by-products in it. You might think that chowing down on lungs, hearts, intestines, and kidneys is disgusting, but your Lab will love it. What's more, high-quality by-products are a better protein source than meat.

The first ingredient on the dog food label should be the protein source, whether it is chicken, by-products, or another meat. Avoid dog foods with meat and bone meal or soy as the first protein source; neither soy nor bone meal is as high quality and digestible as meat or by-products.

Lab Bites

"Can't I just feed my Lab table scraps?" No. Table scraps don't have the nutrition a dog needs. Most table scraps are heavy on carbohydrates, fat, and salt and low on nutrition. They don't provide a balanced diet, either.

Fat

Fat is an energy-dense nutrient at 9 Kilocalories of energy per gram. Animal fat is a high-quality fat source. Dogs and cats use fats that are commonly referred to as Omega-6 long-chained fatty acids. They are usually a mixture of saturated (solid) and unsaturated (liquid) fats. Typical fat sources include beef, poultry, and "animal fat," which may be a mixture of pork, beef, lamb, and horse fat. Animal fats tend to be better than vegetable fats in providing energy.

Lab Bites

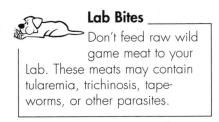

Don't feed raw wild game meat to your Lab. These meats may contain tularemia, trichinosis, tapeworms, or other parasites.

Carbohydrates

Carbohydrates provide 4 Kilocalories of energy per gram. Carbohydrates are useful for adding fiber and extra energy in your Lab's diet. In working dogs, a carbohydrate snack can help refuel a dog's cells after sustained exercise.

Most dogs benefit from cooked grains that are easier to digest. Carbohydrates in the form of fiber help keep your dog's colon healthy and help in water absorption.

Lab Lingo

Tularemia—A bacterial infection that is characterized by high fever, loss of appetite, stiffness, and lethargy.

Trichinosis—A parasitic disease that can cause muscle problems, serious illness, and even death.

Home Cooking

You may be tempted to develop your own diet for your Lab. After all, you probably cook for yourself, so why not cook for your dog, too? Many "home cookers" often cite that the ingredients are fresher and better—free from pesticides, chemicals, preservatives, and fillers. The dogs seem to prefer the home cooking, too.

> **Retriever Rewards**
>
> Feed your Labrador meals instead of free feeding. One benefit to feeding meals is you'll see right away if your Lab is sick. It isn't "okay" for your Lab to skip a meal when he is normally a good eater. It may be a sign of illness.

But how much do you really know about dog nutrition? Do you think you can formulate a complete and balanced diet at home? A lot of research goes into that bag of dog food.

Let's look at some of the proponents' statements in favor of home cooking and my answers to them:

- **Dogs eat meat and vegetables in the wild.** Wolves don't live that long in the wild due to parasites, illness, and injury. Our Labs are far more pampered. In the wild, the wolf doesn't eat "meat and vegetables." The wolf dines on a kill, which includes organ meats, bones, and hair. I've never seen a wolf stalk tofu or a carrot in the wild.
- **The ingredients you use are better and fresher than what is in dog food.** Maybe. Fresh food without preservatives tends to spoil faster. You must be careful about E. coli and Salmonella poisoning. If you cook the food, you might destroy vital nutrients.
- **Wolves eat bones in the wild.** Yes, but no one is around to pay the vet bills if the wolf has a blockage or perforation of the intestines. Bones can be hazardous to your Lab.
- **My dog can't get the nutrition he needs from commercial dog food.** Unless your Lab is sick and needs a special diet (and

there are many veterinary diets available) or if he is an endurance sled dog, he will get all the nutrition he needs from a premium or super-premium dog food. AAFCO has set forth the minimum nutritional guidelines for dog foods. Unless you are a veterinary nutritionist, how close do you think you can come to balancing nutrients? For example, calcium and phosphorus require a special balance of about 1.5 to 1. If phosphorus exceeds that ratio (as in a diet with too much meat), the dog's body will pull calcium from the bones, making them brittle.

- **Feeding raw foods will make my dog healthier.** Maybe. Or it could make him sick. Some foods, such as onions and raw salmon, shouldn't be fed to your Lab under any circumstances. Raw salmon from the Northwest may contain a fluke that can be poisonous to your Lab; onions can cause anemia. Raw game meat can contain tularemia, trichinosis, and tapeworms. There is also the potential for food poisoning due to salmonella and E. coli. If you're set on feeding your Lab a raw food diet or a home-cooked diet, contact a veterinary college and speak with a nutritionist there. Most will be able to recommend and analyze diets for deficiencies.

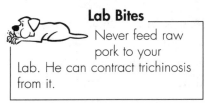

> **Lab Bites**
>
> Never feed raw pork to your Lab. He can contract trichinosis from it.

Performance Diets—Feeding the Canine Athlete

If your Lab works hard, such as in field trials, hunting, agility, or other work, he should be on a super-premium performance blend of dog food. You must be careful when feeding your dog performance foods, though, because the tendency is to feed too much. Your Labrador will swiftly become a "Pigador."

Higher protein and fat is necessary for hardworking dogs to maintain muscle mass and keep weight. When you choose a high-performance dog food, find one that is highly digestible. Otherwise, you may see stress diarrhea or even bloody diarrhea. Some cheaper brands of dog food have rough-cut grains that can irritate your Lab's bowels and cause bleeding. If you see bleeding, have your vet check out your Lab to rule out other causes. If your Lab is in good shape, try mixing water with his food, changing dog foods, or adding canned dog food to his diet to help "cushion" the food as it passes through his intestines.

Lab Bites

If your Lab has diarrhea or bloody diarrhea, it might be stress diarrhea. But before you decide it is stress diarrhea, have your vet check out your Lab to rule out other causes such as parvovirus and parasites. If your Lab is in good health and still shows diarrhea, try switching dog foods, adding water to his dog food, or adding canned dog food.

Obese Dogs

Obesity is a common problem among pets. Many pet owners dole out food with their love and are slowly killing their pets. Being fat isn't any more healthy for your Lab than it is for you.

Your Lab should be neither too thin nor too fat. Weight in pounds isn't a good indicator of fitness because different Labs have different builds. Instead, you should examine your Lab to determine his fitness. You should be able to put your thumbs on his spine and feel his ribs. If you can't feel the ribs, or can barely feel them under a thick layer of padding, your Lab is too fat. If you can see your Lab's ribs and pelvic bones, he is too thin.

Retriever Rewards

If you have a senior dog, you shouldn't necessarily switch your Lab to a senior diet unless he is overweight. Talk with your vet if you have concerns over your Lab's diet.

Retriever Rewards

If you and your Lab are exercising to shed weight, remember the following rules:

- Start slowly; your Lab is probably out of shape and needs to build up to rigorous exercise.
- Choose an activity you both can do that's fun. Playing fetch, jogging, and dog sports are possible activities.
- Be careful when exercising when it's hot. Overweight dogs tend to overheat faster.

You can talk with your vet about putting your Lab on a diet. Most vets are able to prescribe a diet food that will help shed the pounds. If your Lab is the quintessential couch potato, getting him off the couch and into an exercise regimen will help shave off unwanted pounds. You can also try the maintenance or "lite" version of your Lab's food.

What *Not* to Feed Your Lab

Now that you know what's good for your dog, here are some things that are *not* good to feed your dog.

(© Kent and Donna Dannen)

Your Lab puppy will benefit from a balanced diet.

Retriever Rewards

"Ok, so I can't feed my Lab just table scraps. Can I add table scraps to his dinner?" Table scraps can turn a Lab into a picky eater. If you decide to feed table scraps, limit table scraps and other treats to no more than 10 percent of his daily ration.

Junk Food—Table Scraps and Between-Meal Snacks

You should limit snacks, treats, and other goodies to no more than 10 percent of your Lab's total food ration. This includes training treats, table scraps, biscuits, and other snacks (including doggie ice cream!).

I don't recommend feeding table scraps because they can turn your Lab into a picky eater. But if you do feed scraps, keep them small in portion and avoid high-fat, high-sugar, high-carbohydrate, and high-salt portions. Small pieces of boneless cooked meat such as chicken, turkey, steak, and fish are okay as treats, but remember that these treats should make up no more than 10 percent of your Lab's diet.

Retriever Rewards

To teach good eating habits, put down your Lab's bowl with his food and set a timer for 10 minutes. At the end of 10 minutes, pick up his food bowl if he hasn't touched it and don't give him more food until his next feeding time. After a few rounds of this, your Lab will learn that feeding time means time to eat.

Poisonous Temptations—Chocolate and Other Unsafe Foods

Not everything is safe for your Lab to eat. Some foods are poisonous to dogs. These include the following:

- **Chocolate**—Contains theobromine, a substance that is poisonous to dogs. Dark or bittersweet chocolate is more poisonous than milk chocolate.

- **Onions**—May cause anemia.
- **Raw salmon from the Northwest**—Contains a parasite that can kill your Lab.
- **Alcohol**—Even a small amount can cause alcohol poisoning. A drunk Lab is *not* funny, and a small amount can be extremely toxic.

Lab Bites

Avoid feeding your Lab "fad" diets that have strange or unusual ingredients or aren't formulated to AAFCO guidelines. For one thing, diets that aren't formulated to meet or surpass AAFCO guidelines aren't complete and balanced and may cause severe nutritional deficiencies.

The Least You Need to Know

- Feed your Lab a premium dog food that meets or exceeds AAFCO standards in accordance with his age and activity level.
- Homemade diets can be tricky to balance and may cause malnutrition or disease. If you decide to formulate your own dog food, contact a veterinary nutritionist to help you develop a complete and balanced diet.
- Athletic labs and obese dogs require special nutrition.
- Limit snacks and treats to no more than 10 percent of your Lab's total diet. Avoid chocolate and other foods that will poison your dog.

Chapter 17

Healthy Choices—Preventative Care

In This Chapter

- Why should you spay/neuter your Lab?
- How to examine your Labrador Retriever for health problems
- How to keep your Lab's teeth and ears clean
- How to groom your dog
- How to give your Lab medicines

Your Lab will be healthier and happier when you take responsibility for his health. In this chapter, you'll learn about preventative care to keep your Lab healthy and what signs to look for in a sick dog.

You'll also learn the basics of grooming, such as how to keep your Lab's toenails from becoming claws and how to keep those stinky anal sacs clear.

Lastly, you'll learn how to give your Lab medication without a struggle.

The Great Spay/Neuter Debate

Most dog owners have heard that they should spay or neuter their dogs. Still, many don't comply. There are numerous reasons to spay and neuter, including health benefits, but many owners are still under the misconception that spaying and neutering will somehow make their dog less valuable.

Lab Facts

Your Lab will be healthier and happier if he is spayed or neutered before one year. Spaying and neutering reduces or eliminates a number of potential health risks such as ovarian cancer, mammary tumors, and pyometra in females; and testicular cancer and anal tumors in males.

Unless your Lab is a show dog or competes professionally in field trials, there is really no reason to keep him intact.

Common Misconceptions

Let's talk about some of the common myths and misconceptions surrounding spaying and neutering:

- **My dog will miss sex.** The truth is that sex is a purely instinctual drive in a dog and they don't get any pleasure or enjoyment from it. Breeding isn't pleasurable; it's instinctual. And it can be downright painful for them.
- **My female should have a litter of puppies to enhance her maternal instincts.** Some females do go through behavior changes after having puppies, but not necessarily for the better. Females who don't have puppies don't think about having puppies, nor do they miss them.

- **My male dog will be less aggressive and less protective.** First of all, Labs aren't *supposed* to be aggressive. If you're looking for an aggressive, protective dog, look at another breed, not the Labrador Retriever! Protectiveness varies according to the individual dog and the bond between the owner and dog. Spaying or neutering will help your dog focus on you and not instinctive drives.
- **My Lab will get fat and lazy.** Overeating and lack of exercise cause your Lab to get fat and lazy, not neutering and spaying. Some dogs do become more interested in food after neutering and spaying, so you may have to cut back the rations a bit. But the bright side is that you'll save on dog food.
- **It's healthier for a female to have a litter of puppies.** Actually, it's not. If you spay a female while she's young, you decrease the risk of mammary tumors and eliminate a life-threatening disease called pyometra.
- **My Lab won't act male.** Actually, he will. It's a little-known fact that neutered males will try to mate with females in season and will succeed—but they won't reproduce. Neutered males may take a little extra time to lift their legs, but they eventually do. Neutering will actually make a young dog bigger because it causes the growth plates (that is, the bones that grow) to close later.

Why You Should Spay or Neuter Your Lab

Every year, approximately five million pets show up in shelters, many of them purebred dogs and many of those Labrador Retrievers. Spaying or neutering could help reduce this problem.

Many owners fail to spay or neuter their dogs because they are purebreds. If you've read this book, you know that being purebred doesn't make the dog any more valuable than any other. Then, one little accident and the dog has puppies. Often, they're not purebred.

Lab Facts

Your spayed or neutered Lab may compete in all performance competitions with the exception of conformation shows and professional field trials.

Although you may find homes for these puppies, it takes away potential homes for other mixed breeds. And how many homes actually keep the dog through its entire life? Did you screen them thoroughly? The truth is, you've just added to the pet overpopulation problem.

Behavior and Health Benefits

There are other reasons for spaying and neutering your Lab, namely health and behavioral. You may be surprised to learn that spaying and neutering helps improve your dog's temperament. Dogs who are spayed and neutered tend to focus more on you than on the mating drive. With a spayed female, there's no estrus, meaning that you don't have to cloister her away for a month twice a year. With males, you're not fighting the sometimes overpowering drive to look for females in season. If you have a multi-dog household, you may see less aggression if all the dogs are spayed and neutered. I've seen a remarkable turnaround with my dogs after spaying and neutering—even with the females.

Neutered males are less likely to develop anal tumors. Neutering eliminates testicular cancer as well. Spayed females are less likely to develop mammary tumors if spayed before two years old and won't develop ovarian and uterine cancers. They also won't develop pyometra, a life-threatening infection of the uterus.

The Health Exam—How to Examine Your Lab

You should make it a weekly ritual to examine your Lab, preferably while grooming him. Start with your Lab's head and work your way back. Look for abnormalities such as bumps and lumps.

Here are some specific items to check:

- **Eyes**—Your Lab's eyes should be clear and bright without excessive or pus-like discharge. There should be no redness or tearing.
- **Nose**—Your Lab's nose should be cool to the touch and moist. A hot and dry nose may indicate a fever. There should be no discharge or blood.
- **Ears**—Your Lab's ears should be clean and sweet smelling. Any foul odor or excessive buildup of wax indicates a potential ear problem.
- **Mouth**—Your Lab's teeth should be white and clean, without a tartar buildup. Your Lab's breath should not be foul smelling. If it is, it may suggest tooth or gum problems. Are the gums a healthy pink (or black due to pigment), or are they red or swollen?
- **Legs**—Feel down your Lab's legs to check for any lumps or bumps. Inspect the footpads for cuts and foreign objects such as *foxtails*. Look at the toenails—they shouldn't be red or broken. If you find an unusual bump, check the other side to see if it is normal or if it is only on one side. If the bump is unilateral, it might be a tumor. Check the legs for full range of motion, moving them slowly and gently in full range. There should be no clicks or pops.
- **Skin and fur**—Are there any sores, bald patches, or redness to the skin? Is the skin dry or flaky? Are there dark grains through the fur that turn red when wet?
- **Tail**—Is the tail healthy looking or hanging limp? Has your Lab been chewing on it?

Lab Lingo

Foxtails—Also called grass awns, these sticky seeds burrow into a dog's coat and skin. They can bury themselves into the body, causing abscesses.

Retriever Rewards

Examine your Lab thoroughly at least once a week to spot potential health problems.

- **Sex organs**—Is there discharge from the vagina or penis? (In intact female dogs, however, discharge is normal during estrus.)

Pearly Whites—Keeping the Doggie Dentist at Bay

Doggie dentistry may sound humorous, but it's serious business. Infected teeth can cause severe health problems, including heart problems. Professional teeth cleaning requires anesthesia and its associated risks—not to mention the expense!

Many vets recommend brushing your dog's teeth every day with a toothpaste specially formulated for dogs. Quite honestly, most dog owners don't have the time or patience to do that, so I recommend brushing your Lab's teeth once a week to reduce plaque, which leads to tartar. If your Lab has good teeth (and healthy teeth and gums largely depend on genetics and diet), you might be able to get away with brushing his teeth less, but that's inadvisable.

> **Lab Bites**
> Never use human toothpaste on dogs. Human toothpaste contains fluoride and other ingredients that are exceedingly toxic to dogs. Brush your Lab's teeth only with toothpaste approved for dogs.

Brushing Your Lab's Teeth

Naturally, your Lab is first going to have to become used to you handling his mouth. Start by holding your Lab's head gently and flipping up his lip and touching his teeth and gums. Do this gently and praise him. Practice this often so that he becomes used to you touching his mouth.

After he becomes used to you handling his mouth, get a soft washcloth and wet a corner of it. Now, with your finger, gently massage your Lab's gums with the tip of the washcloth.

The next step is to get a toothbrush designed for dogs. Use toothpaste formulated for pets. (Never use human toothpaste; it's poisonous to dogs.) Most dog toothpastes are chicken or malt flavored, so the taste is appealing. Your Lab doesn't have to rinse and spit!

Lab Facts

The condition of a dog's teeth largely depends on genetics and diet. I've seen dogs with horrible-looking teeth improve dramatically once they were put on a premium diet. I've seen other dogs that, despite the premium diet, had thin enamel and bad teeth. You can still make a difference in the health of your Lab's teeth by brushing them regularly.

Recognizing a Tooth or Gum Problem

Hopefully, your Lab will go through life without a tooth or gum problem. If you feed him good nutrition and give him plenty of chewing toys, you should minimize the need for teeth cleaning. However, your Lab may still have a tooth or gum problem. The following potential warning signs suggest that it's time to visit the vet:

- Loss of appetite
- Sudden, unexpected chewing on inappropriate items
- Bad breath
- Nasal discharge
- Red, swollen gums
- A lump above or below a particular tooth

Do You Hear What I Hear?

Labs frequently develop ear infections due to their hanging ears. Their ears make an ideal place for bacteria to grow and mites to hide. Keep your Lab's ears clean.

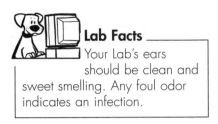

> **Lab Facts**
> Your Lab's ears should be clean and sweet smelling. Any foul odor indicates an infection.

Cleaning Your Lab's Ears

Use a mild otic solution for dogs. Squeeze some into your Lab's ears and then gently massage the outside of the ear canal. Now take sterile gauze or sponges and gently wipe out the excess.

Recognizing an Ear Problem

These are the signs of potential ear problems, which suggest that it's time to visit the vet:

- Your Lab scratches at, paws, or shakes his head.
- Foul-smelling odor coming from the ears.
- Excessive waxy buildup.
- Ears are crusty or red.
- Red or black waxy buildup.

Grooming Your Lab

So far, I've been touting the Lab as a wash-and-wear dog—and with good reason. Labs are low maintenance when it comes to grooming. Still, there are some basic things you need to do.

The Lab Coat

Labs do shed, so don't think that your Lab is a "no maintenance" dog. Labs do have an undercoat that keeps them warm in winter. (They're from Newfoundland originally, remember?) When your Lab sheds, you may see tufts of fur protruding from his guard hairs, which you can easily comb out. Your Lab may have certain times of the year that he sheds, or he might simply shed a bit year round.

Not surprisingly, you may find your Lab's coat naturally oily. These oils help protect the Lab's skin and coat from Newfoundland waters. Use a Zoom Groom or other comb to remove the dead hair and evenly distribute those oils. You should brush against the natural lay of the coat to further loosen and remove dead hair and stimulate the coat's natural oils. Use a slicker brush for removing undercoat and excessive hair. Then, brush the coat back to its normal lay.

Retriever Rewards

A recent phenomenon is do-it-yourself dog washes. These facilities provide grooming-style tubs, water, soaps, towels, grooming tables, and blow dryers, making bathing your Lab a breeze. It also keeps the mess there and not in your home!

Baths

You usually don't need to bathe your Lab unless he is dirty or has been swimming. If your Lab swims in a pool, the chlorine can damage his coat if it's not rinsed out. Salt water may also damage a coat, so be sure to give your Lab a bath after taking a dip.

Retriever Rewards

You need to bathe, or at least rinse off, your Lab after he goes swimming, to remove chlorine or salt water from his fur so that it won't damage his fur or irritate his skin.

Dog shampoos and rinses are specially balanced for your dog's skin, so don't be afraid to use them. Don't use human shampoos; they are formulated for humans—not dogs—and will strip the oils from your Lab's coat.

Retriever Rewards

Always rinse your Lab until the water runs clean—excessive soap attracts dirt and may irritate your Lab's skin.

When you give your Lab a bath, do so in a warm place, away from drafts. Always comb and brush out your Lab first to remove excess dirt and hair. Then soak your Lab with tepid water, lather him up, and rinse well. Apply a creme rinse, if desired, and rinse thoroughly. Always rinse your Lab thoroughly to avoid skin irritation.

Tap Dancing—Clipping Your Lab's Toenails

The screaming. The carrying on. You'd think you were torturing the poor dog! Actually, you're just clipping his toenails. It doesn't have to be this way, but quite often, it is. Dogs hate having their toenails clipped, and Labs are no exception. One problem is that many Labs have black toenails, which makes clipping a tap dance. Still, you need to clip your Lab's nails once a week to keep them short and healthy. Long nails may break and cause pain.

Dogs have a pink part where the nerves and blood supply to the nail are, called the *quick*. Because many Labs' nails are dark, you have to make an educated guess where the quick is. If you cut into the quick, your Lab will let you know in no uncertain terms—and won't want you near his paws again! He'll also bleed profusely.

Lab Lingo

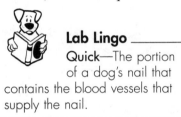

Quick—The portion of a dog's nail that contains the blood vessels that supply the nail.

When you start clipping your Lab's nails, use a dog nail clipper (either a guillotine or scissors action) and snip off a small portion of the nail at a time to trim back the nails. If the nail feels "spongy" or hard to cut, stop immediately. You can use a nail grinder, which will help file away the nail instead. Some dogs handle the nail grinder better than the clippers.

Have "styptic powder" or sodium nitrate on hand, in case you do cut the quick. Packing the nail with styptic powder will stop the bleeding. You can buy styptic powder at pet-supply stores or through pet-supply catalogs. In a pinch, cornstarch will do.

Anal Sacs

A dog has two glands at the four and eight o'clock positions around the anus. These usually empty themselves when the dog defecates, but occasionally they become overfull or impacted.

If your Lab starts scooting around on his rear or chewing the fur on his rear or tail, he may have full or impacted anal sacs. The best times to empty these are when you are bathing him. These are smellier than a skunk and you'll want to clean him off after you express them.

Fold up a wad of paper towels and place them over your Lab's anus. Now press gently on the four and eight o'clock positions. The glands should express themselves. Don't put your face near them while you are pressing against them or you'll be in for a nasty surprise. Be certain to cover the entire anus because they squirt.

If the problem persists, bring your Lab to the vet. The dog could have impacted anal glands, which your vet may have to express.

Retriever Rewards

The best time to express your Lab's anal sacs is during a bath.

Giving Medications

Occasionally, your vet may ask you to administer medications to your Lab. The most frequent are pills, but occasionally you may have to give liquids.

It helps if your Lab is comfortable with you handling his mouth. Start at an early age to get him used to you touching his mouth. (Brushing his teeth is an ideal time for this.) Once your Lab is used to you touching his mouth, giving medications is less stressful.

Pill Popping

People seem to have a hard time giving pills. The truth is, practice makes perfect. Most dogs will swallow a pill readily if you open their mouths, pop the pill into the back of their mouths, and close their jaws with their head tilted upward. Stroking the underside of the throat helps too. Some pet owners use a little device called a pet piller. It does the same thing, only a little more accurately. So if your aim to the back of the throat is lousy, try one of these.

If you can't get the hang of this, try hiding the pill in peanut butter. Most dogs love peanut butter; it sticks to the roof of their mouth—which provides hours of entertainment for the owner—and gets the pill down without a fuss. An alternative is to hide the pill in a piece of hot dog (do they even taste it?) or some other treat. If the pill can be ground up (some can't—check with your vet), try mixing it with one of his meals. Always check with your veterinarian whether the medication can be given with food or should be given on an empty stomach.

Liquid Medications

Liquid medications are fairly easy to administer. Ask your vet for an oral syringe with the amount marked on the syringe in permanent marker. Fill the syringe and then pull out your Lab's lower lip, near where it joins the upper lip, to form a pouch. Squirt the medication gently into the pouch, release it, and tilt your Lab's head back. If you're giving a lot of liquid, you need to administer it slowly so that the dog has time to swallow.

The Least You Need to Know

- Your Lab will be healthier and better behaved, and will not contribute to pet overpopulation, if he or she is neutered or spayed.
- Examine your Lab at least once a week for signs of illness and abnormalities.
- Keep your Lab's ears clean and free from infections by cleaning his ears with a mild otic solution.

- Brush your Lab's teeth once a week with a toothpaste formulated for dogs.
- Labs need brushing once or twice weekly to promote good coat health. Wash him when he is dirty or has been swimming. You also need to clip his toenails and keep his anal sac clean.
- Try mixing the medication with your dog's food or hiding it in a treat if you have trouble giving medications.

Chapter 18

To Your Dog's Health

In This Chapter

- Learn which congenital and hereditary diseases might affect your Lab
- Common ailments and injuries that can affect your Lab and what to do
- What to do when emergencies happen

Labs are the most popular of the AKC breeds. Unfortunately, their popularity brings with it hereditary diseases due to poor breeding practices and failure to screen for hereditary diseases. In this chapter, you'll learn the most common of the hereditary diseases found in Labs.

You'll also learn which ailments and injuries are common in dogs and how to recognize and treat them and when to call the vet.

You'll learn about potential emergencies and how to treat your Lab to give her the best possible chance when you bring her to the emergency room.

Hereditary and Congenital Diseases

The Labrador Retriever is a popular dog. Unfortunately, popularity has its price. Many Labs have *hereditary* and *congenital* conditions. Sadly, many cases of hip dysplasia, elbow dysplasia, and other hereditary diseases could have been avoided if the breeders had vigilantly screened for these diseases.

(© Kent and Donna Dannen)

Four healthy Labs in the three Lab colors: Black, Chocolate, and two shades of Yellow.

Many of these diseases, such as hip dysplasia, tricuspid valve disease, and epilepsy, severely affect your Lab's quality of life. This is why it's imperative that you purchase your Lab from a reputable breeder.

Lab Lingo

Congenital—A condition that is present at birth and may have either genetic or environmental causes.

Hereditary—A condition that is genetic; that is, inherited through the genes of the parents.

Bloat—a Life-Threatening Condition

Bloat—also called gastric torsion, gastric dilatation, or canine gastric dilatation-volvulus (CGDV)—is a severe, life-threatening condition. It affects many deep-chested breeds, including Labs; structure seems to be the main determinant as to whether the dog will bloat.

The afflicted dog's stomach fills with gas and fluid. More than just an upset stomach, the dog's stomach fills so much that it begins to twist on its axis. This terrible twisting damages the stomach, esophagus, and intestines and shuts off blood supply to those organs. When the stomach twists, the condition then is called gastric torsion or gastric dilatation-volvulus (CGDV). The dog will go into shock and will die a painful death if untreated.

Retriever Rewards

The best treatment for bloat is to prevent it. Here are some tips:

- Feed him several smaller meals rather than one big one.
- Wet down your Lab's food (don't let it sit long) to encourage quick evacuation from the stomach. Tests show that food with water poured over it leaves the stomach less than an hour after eating.
- Don't change dog foods or give snacks that cause digestive upset.
- Don't exercise your Lab after he has eaten.
- Encourage slower eating. Some people have gone as far as to put fist-size stones (too big for their Lab to swallow) in their dogs' bowls to encourage them to slow down.
- Don't allow garbage raids, counter raids, or other snacking—intentional or unintentional.

Bloat occurs up to three hours after eating. Your Lab will suddenly look pregnant or fat. He may pace back and forth and look uncomfortable. He may drool and attempt to vomit without success. If your Lab shows these symptoms after eating, don't attempt to treat him yourself! Get him to the vet as soon as possible.

> **Lab Bites**
>
> Watch for signs of bloat: suddenly looking fat or "pregnant," pacing and drooling, discomfort when sitting or lying down, and retching and attempts at vomiting without producing anything. This is a life-threatening condition—seek veterinary assistance immediately.

Cold Tail

Cold tail or cold-water tail is a condition in which your Lab's tail becomes limp—almost as though it were paralyzed. Labs seem to be predisposed to this. It occurs usually after swimming in a cold lake or water. The tail stands straight out for three or four inches and then hangs down as if broken. It is painful, but it usually gets better after a few days.

It can happen after vigorous exercising as well. The cause is still unknown, but studies tend to suggest that the culprit is damaged tail muscles.

Elbow Dysplasia (ED) and Osteochondritis Dissecans (OCD)

Elbow dysplasia is a hereditary disease where the elbow joints are malformed. This disease is called *polygenic* because several genes may cause it. Although osteochondritis dissecans (OCD) can be due to trauma, when it is paired with elbow dysplasia, it is most likely due to hereditary conditions. OCD is a disease of the cartilage covering the ends of the bones. OCD can be very painful, causing a cartilage flap to form over the elbow. That flap may tear or reattach, which requires surgery to have it removed.

Elbow dysplasia is not usually screened for in Labs. Between 1974 and 1999, only 11,115 were tested for elbow dysplasia, and a little more than 12 percent of those tested as dysplastic; however, statistics suggest that the actual percentage of dogs with the disease is much higher.

Surgery, anti-inflammatories, and *nutriceuticals* are recommended treatments for elbow dysplasia. Obviously, surgery can be very expensive and arthritis often sets in to the joints, further complicating matters. You should never breed a dog with elbow dysplasia so that you can avoid passing it on.

Lab Lingo

Polygenic—A trait or condition coming from more than one gene pair.

Nutriceuticals—A nutritional supplement intended to help mitigate a condition or disease.

Epilepsy

Epilepsy exists in all breeds and mixed breeds. It is usually hereditary in dogs and quite prevalent in some lines. Studies show that some Labrador Retrievers have a genetic predisposition to epilepsy. "Idiopathic" epilepsy (epilepsy where the specific cause is not known) in dogs is very similar to epilepsy in humans. However, other causes of epilepsy must be ruled out before declaring the condition to be "idiopathic." This includes trauma to the head, poisoning, tick paralysis, parasites, deficiencies in certain vitamins, overheating, intestinal obstructions, liver problems, and calcium imbalances.

If your Lab is epileptic, your vet will need to perform some tests to rule out other causes. If the seizures are frequent or become worse, your vet usually will prescribe a medication to help control the seizures. You should never breed a dog with epilepsy.

Eye Diseases

Progressive Retinal Atrophy (PRA) and Central Progressive Retinal Atrophy (CPRA) are two degenerative eye disorders that lead to blindness. Cataracts or cloudiness of the eye's lens can be due to either hereditary or environmental reasons. Juvenile cataracts are usually hereditary. A veterinary ophthalmologist can determine whether your Lab has these or other eye diseases.

The Canine Eye Registry Foundation (CERF) provides a registry for dogs intended for breeding. The CERF evaluation lasts for one year. Any Lab you buy should have both its parents registered with CERF. If you plan to breed your Lab, you will need to have his eyes examined and have him registered with CERF.

Hip Dysplasia (HD)

Hip dysplasia is a crippling genetic disease. No amount of good nutrition and care will stop it. It is caused by the malformation of the hip socket. In mildly dysplastic cases, your vet may be able to help mitigate the effects with nutriceuticals such as glucosamine, chondroitin, and creatine and anti-inflammatories such as aspirin. Some cases are so bad that the dog must have surgery. In some extreme cases, the dog must be euthanized.

The OFA statistics don't tell the whole tale here. Between 1974 and 2000, only 125,214 Labrador Retrievers were tested for hip dysplasia—not even equal to the number registered in one year! Talk to any reputable breeder, rescue worker, or vet and they'll tell you that hip dysplasia is prevalent in Labrador Retrievers.

Lab Bites

Hip dysplasia is a devastating disease. Many dogs who have it are in such pain that they need surgery or, in some cases, euthanasia. This is why it is vitally important to have your Lab's parents checked for sound hips. Don't take the breeder's word for it; ask for proof. Don't feel embarrassed. Reputable breeders will be happy to show you proof.

Surgery is extremely expensive, costing thousands of dollars in most cases. This is why it is very important to purchase your Lab from a reputable breeder. You should never breed a dog with hip dysplasia or without an OFA rating of GOOD or EXCELLENT hips.

Hypothyroidism

Hypothyroidism occurs when the dog's thyroid produces insufficient thyroid hormone. Symptoms can include lethargy, dull and dry coat, obesity or weight gain, and a thinning haircoat. The dog may seek warmer areas. Hypothyroidism can cause infertility in intact males and females.

Some forms of hypothyroidism may be hereditary, so it is inadvisable to breed a hypothyroid dog. Your vet can diagnose hypothyroidism through a blood test. If your Lab is hypothyroid, your veterinarian may prescribe a form of thyroid hormone. OFA has a relatively new thyroid registry. Breeders should test and register their Labs with the OFA.

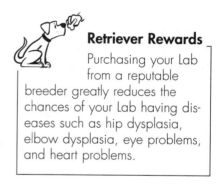

Retriever Rewards

Purchasing your Lab from a reputable breeder greatly reduces the chances of your Lab having diseases such as hip dysplasia, elbow dysplasia, eye problems, and heart problems.

Hereditary Myopathy of Labrador Retrievers (HMLR)

Labrador Retriever Myopathy is a muscle disorder found in Labs in which the dog has a marked deficiency of muscle mass due to a deficiency of Type II muscle fibers. This condition is found only in Labrador Retrievers. The condition starts showing signs when the puppy is three or four months old. The puppy may be weak and have a stiff, hopping gait. He may collapse after what would be considered normal exercise.

Cold weather and stress may aggravate symptoms and cause collapse. The severity of the condition varies and usually stabilizes by the time the puppy is six months to one year old. Obviously, puppies with this condition can't work, although they can be pets. Further studies are being done on this disease and there may be a blood test soon to detect carriers of this disease.

Paneosteitis

Paneosteitis or "Pano" is a condition where a growing puppy suddenly becomes lame. This lameness may be mild to severe and may affect different parts of the puppy at different times. The onset of Pano is somewhere around 5 to 12 months and usually affects males more than females. Large and giant breeds are usually affected by "Pano." It may or may not have a genetic component.

If your puppy has "Pano," your veterinarian may prescribe analgesics and rest. He may ask you to limit exercise. Eventually, as the puppy gets older, the pain subsides and the puppy grows out of it.

Tricuspid Valve Dysplasia (TVD)

Tricuspid Valve Dysplasia (TVD) is a heart condition found in Labrador Retrievers. Puppies are born with this condition and it appears to be hereditary. With TVD, the tricuspid valve in the heart is deformed, causing the valve not to close tightly. The blood leaks from the valve into the right atrium of the heart, causing the right side of the heart to enlarge. TVD can be mild to severe. Puppies with mild TVD can live somewhat normal lives, but puppies with severe TVD will die before they reach a year.

The mode of inheritance isn't known yet, but researchers are looking into TVD. To avoid TVD, buy a puppy from parents who are registered with the OFA Cardiac database or the Genetic Disease Control in Animals (GDC) database.

Illnesses and Injuries

Even though you may take good care of your Lab, there's still the chance that he will contract some type of illness or injury during his life. It's inevitable. I'll cover some of the most common problems dog owners face.

Allergies

Ah-choo! We all think of hay fever when we talk about allergies. You might be surprised to hear that dogs get it, too. But there are also other types of allergies as well, including allergies to certain external (contact) exposure and to food.

Some contact allergies are apparent; some aren't as easy to diagnose. For example, if your Lab's skin looks irritated and is itchy after using a particular shampoo, you might guess that the dog is allergic to a chemical in that shampoo. However, you might not know why your Lab's nose and face are swollen and irritated. Many dogs are allergic to plastic or rubber and may react to the plastic bowls you feed them out of. Most contact-allergy diagnoses are based on the owner's observations.

Lab Facts

You may be surprised to learn that lamb isn't any better for a dog than any other type of meat. Lamb was originally used in hypoallergenic diets because dogs had little exposure to lamb meat. However, as more people have fed their dogs lamb and rice diets (thinking that they were better), vets have been seeing allergies to lamb! Lamb is no longer considered a novel protein source for dogs.

Labs can be allergic to certain ingredients in their food such as corn or wheat, or the protein source, such as beef, soy, or lamb. These types of allergies manifest themselves with digestive upsets and skin problems.

Dietary allergies are a bit tricky to diagnose. Your vet will recommend a hypoallergenic diet for several weeks. This diet usually has a novel protein source—that is, a protein source that dogs generally don't eat such as fish, venison, or even kangaroo meat. It may have an unusual carbohydrate source too, such as potatoes. After your dog is on this diet several weeks , you add the potential problem ingredients to determine what the allergy is. Some dog owners are so relieved to have their dogs free from the allergy that they keep them on the hypoallergenic diet.

Lab Facts

Flea Bite Dermatitis or Flea Allergy Dermatitis is caused by your Lab's allergic reaction to—you guessed it—fleas (actually, flea saliva). Eliminate the fleas and you eliminate the allergy.

Broken Toenails

Your Lab may experience cracked or broken toenails, especially if you allow them to grow too long. Trim the toenail and file off any rough edges if the toenail has broken below the quick (the blood supply to the nail). If the nail is bleeding, you can stop the bleeding with styptic powder, silver nitrate, or an electric nail cauterizer available through pet supply mail-order catalogs. You can then paint the nail with a skin bond agent, which is available from your veterinarian or through veterinary supply houses.

Diarrhea and Vomiting

Changes in diet, overeating, strange water, and nervousness can cause diarrhea, but so can parvovirus, internal parasites, rancid food, allergies, and other serious ailments. If your Lab is dehydrated, has a fever (over 102°F), or has extreme or bloody diarrhea, bring him to your vet as soon as possible.

If your Lab has mild diarrhea (soft stools—not liquid and without mucus), does not have dehydration, and is not vomiting, you can give him a kaolin product (Kaopectate) or a bismuth subsalicylate product (Pepto-Bismol). Give 1 to 2 teaspoons Kaopectate per 10 pounds body weight every 4 hours, or 1 to 2 teaspoons Pepto-Bismol per 10 pounds body weight every 12 hours. Withhold your Lab's next meal to see whether the diarrhea improves. Encourage your Lab to drink water or an unflavored pediatric electrolyte solution. If there is no diarrhea or vomiting, you can feed him a mixture of boiled hamburger and rice at the next meal. If your Lab's condition does not improve or becomes worse, contact your veterinarian.

Dogs vomit for a variety of reasons. Dogs sometimes eat grass and then vomit. Dogs also vomit due to obstructions, an enlarged esophagus, parvovirus and other serious illnesses, allergies, and rancid food. If your Lab vomits more than once or twice, projectile vomits, starts becoming dehydrated, has severe diarrhea along with vomiting, has a fever (over 102°F), or retches without vomiting, bring him to the veterinarian immediately.

Lab Facts

Occasionally your vet will require you to take your Lab's temperature. Purchase an electronic rectal thermometer. Wash the thermometer with soapy water and sterilize it with isopropyl alcohol. Use petroleum jelly as a lubricant and gently insert the thermometer into your Lab's rectum. Hold your Lab quietly for about two minutes to obtain a reading. Do not allow your dog to sit down or he might break the thermometer or push it farther into the rectum. Normal temperatures for Labs are 100.5°F to 102°F.

Foxtails

Foxtails, or grass awns, are seeds from grass-like plants. They have a sharp, burrowing head with a tail that looks like a fox's tail (hence the name). These seeds have a nasty habit of getting into your Lab's fur and ears. With each movement, they burrow into the dog's skin.

Check your Lab thoroughly after he's been outside for burrs and foxtails. Check his ears too. I've seen foxtails bury themselves deeply into a dog's skin. They can cause abscesses and can even enter organs.

Retriever Rewards

Check your Lab after every time he's been in the field. Foxtails or grass awns can burrow their way into a dog's skin and cause dangerous abscesses. Foxtails have been known to burrow through skin into organs. These are nasty seeds that can do a lot of damage.

If you find a partially buried foxtail, use tweezers to pull it out and watch for signs of infection. Take your Lab to the vet if you see pus, swelling, or redness around the site.

Hot Spots

"Hot spots" are areas of moist dermatitis (skin inflammation) that may become infected. The symptoms are reddening skin, missing hair, and oozing wound-like lesions. Allergy, matted fur, or some other form of irritation frequently causes them. Shave or clip all hair surrounding the hot spot and clean twice daily with a 10 percent Betadine/90 percent water solution. If the hot spots are too painful, infected, or extensive, your vet may have to anesthetize your Lab to shave the area and prescribe corticosteroids and antibiotics.

Lumps and Bumps on the Skin

Most lumps are usually benign. However, you should show any lump or bump to your veterinarian. Lumps that are oozing, red, dark-colored, irregular in size and shape, or swiftly growing may be serious; show them to your vet immediately. If your female Lab has lumps on her mammary glands, they may be cancerous mammary tumors requiring surgery. A large doughy lump on the stomach might be a hernia that your vet may have to fix.

Lab Bites

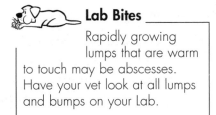

Rapidly growing lumps that are warm to touch may be abscesses. Have your vet look at all lumps and bumps on your Lab.

Rapidly growing lumps may be a form of abscess or infection. Abscesses occur when foreign bodies enter the skin (such as foxtails) or an injury closes with bacteria inside. Abscesses are serious. Your vet must drain the abscess and prescribe antibiotics. Do not attempt to drain the abscess yourself; the wound may become more infected.

Incontinence

Incontinence is generally a sign of a more serious problem such as a bladder or urinary tract infection or bladder stones. Have your vet examine your Lab to determine the cause of incontinence.

Occasionally, spayed female dogs "dribble" and may require medication to correct this.

If your Lab crouches down and urinates when you yell at him or touch him, it may be a form of submissive urination. This is a sign that he respects your authority and is submissive. Some dogs are more submissive than others. Scolding or yelling at your Lab will only aggravate the problem. You can stop this behavior by remaining calm and speaking quietly. Pet your Lab under the chin gently and don't act angry. Most dogs who are overly submissive may require some gentle confidence builders such as clicker training (see Chapter 10) and other positive-reinforcement techniques.

Pyometra—a Life-Threatening Condition for Intact Females

Pyometra is a life-threatening infection of the uterus in intact female dogs. It usually occurs about five or six weeks after the female's last estrus or season. It may come on very suddenly and without warning. Symptoms may be lethargy, refusal to eat, excessive thirst, vomiting, and high temperature. If the cervix is open, you will see a huge amount of blood and pus. If the cervix is closed, you may not see a discharge.

Retriever Rewards

Spaying your Lab will prevent the life-threatening condition called pyometra.

This is a very serious condition. I have lost a female due to this disease and I've known others who have as well. No one knows precisely what causes it, other than a hormone imbalance. The usual treatment is a spay, but sometimes the female is so weak that it can still kill her. Sometimes vets are able to treat an open pyometra with prostaglandin and antibiotics.

This is yet another reason to spay your female Lab. If you aren't showing in conformation or working her in field trials, spay your Lab.

Skunks

There isn't much worse than getting skunked. But before you go and buy out the local supermarket's stock of tomato juice, save your money. You'll just get a stinky pink dog. Purchase a good commercial skunk-odor remover or use the do-it-yourself baking soda/hydrogen peroxide remedy (see the "Retriever Rewards" box).

Retriever Rewards

The famous baking soda/hydrogen peroxide solution for getting rid of skunk odor:

- 1 quart hydrogen peroxide
- 1/4 cup baking soda
- 1 tsp. of shampoo or liquid soap

Wash the dog with this and rinse thoroughly. Don't get any in your Lab's eyes. Don't save any of it in a container—it might explode.

Emergencies

Try as we might to make our dog's lives safer, you might still have an emergency crop up from time to time. Keep your vet's after-hours phone number or the local emergency vet's phone number handy just in case.

Don't panic in an emergency. Panicking wastes precious time you can use to save your dog. Remember that your dog is in pain and scared—he may snap or bite, even at you.

Assembling a First-Aid Kit

Having a first-aid kit for your Lab is important. You can assemble one from easily purchasable items:

- Aspirin
- Bandage scissors
- Bandage tape
- Betadine solution
- Cortisone cream
- Disposable Latex gloves
- An emergency veterinary hospital's phone number
- Hydrogen peroxide
- Kaolin product (Kaopectate)
- Large and small nonstick bandage pads
- Local poison-control center phone number
- Mineral oil
- Petroleum jelly (Vaseline)
- Pressure bandages
- Quick muzzle
- Rectal thermometer
- Self-adhesive wrap (VetWrap or Elastaplast)
- Sterile gauze wrappings
- Sterile sponges

- Surgical glue or VetBond (available through veterinary-supply catalogs)
- Syrup of ipecac
- Triple antibiotic ointment or nitrofurizone (available through veterinary-supply catalogs)
- Tweezers
- Unflavored pediatric electrolyte (Pedialyte)
- Your veterinarian's phone number, pager, or after-hours number

> **Retriever Rewards**
>
> Always have your vet's number, the number to the local poison control center, and the nearest 24-hour emergency vet clinic number taped to your phone, just in case.

Know How to Muzzle Your Lab

In an emergency, you may have to muzzle your Lab. Even the gentlest dog may bite if frightened or injured. Have a quick muzzle (sold in pet-supply stores and through mail order) available. If you don't have one, you can fashion a makeshift muzzle from a bandage, a rope, a belt, or a tie.

Follow these steps:

1. Start in the middle at the bottom of the dog's muzzle.
2. Wrap the bandage upward, tie, and then bring it back downward under the chin and tie.
3. Take the two loose ends and tie them behind the dog's head securely.

> **Lab Bites**
>
> Do not muzzle a dog who is having problems breathing!

Broken Bones or Hit by a Car

Fractures to the head, chest, or back may be life threatening. Use a stiff board to transport the dog (slide the board under the dog) and seek immediate veterinary attention. If your dog has broken his leg, you can fashion a splint from a stick, a rolled-up piece of stiff cardboard, or even a rolled-up newspaper. Put the splint alongside the broken leg and wrap either VetWrap or tape around it. Transport your dog to the veterinarian as soon as possible.

Burns

A severe burn, where the skin is charred or where underlying tissue is exposed, requires immediate veterinary attention. You can treat minor burns over a small area with ice packs or cold water. Do not use water on extensive burns or you may risk shock. Aloe vera is a good burn treatment after the burn has blistered.

Choking or Difficulty Breathing

Signs of choking and breathing difficulty include gagging, coughing, gums and tongue turning pale or blue, and wheezing. Do not muzzle your dog. Loosen your dog's collar and anything else that might restrict breathing. Check your Lab's throat for any object caught in the throat. If you see something that you can remove with tweezers, do so. Do not use your fingers; you can accidentally push the item farther down. If the item is lodged in the throat, try pushing on the dog's abdomen to expel the object. Seek immediate veterinary attention.

If the dog is not breathing, give it mouth-to-mouth resuscitation by closing the dog's mouth and breathing into its nose. Ask your veterinarian how to perform mouth-to-mouth resuscitation correctly, as well as CPR.

Retriever Rewards

Ask your vet to show you the proper way to perform CPR on a dog.

Cuts, Injuries, and Dog Bites

You can clean minor cuts and scrapes yourself with a 10 percent Betadine/90 percent water solution. Then apply a triple antibiotic ointment and watch for signs of infection.

For deep puncture wounds, determine how deep the puncture is. If the object is still embedded, do not remove if practical and seek immediate veterinary treatment. If the puncture is a dog bite that is not serious, you can clean the wound with a Betadine/water solution. Your veterinarian might want to prescribe antibiotics to prevent infection. Be certain that both your dog and the biting dog have had their current rabies vaccinations.

Retriever Rewards

You think your Lab is pregnant. Perhaps you caught the neighborhood mutt with her, or perhaps she's been putting on a bit of weight lately and you've started counting back and it's been about 60-some-odd days since her last season.

If your Lab is not competing in conformation dog shows, bring her down to the vet for a spay. This is the safest way to prevent an unwanted pregnancy. You *were* meaning to do it, weren't you? If your Lab is showing in conformation, it gets a little tricky. So-called mismate shots or morning-after shots can terminate the pregnancy at early stages, but there is a high probability of endangering the dog's life.

If your Lab is getting chunky and her nipples are starting to drop, she's due at any time. You might as well resign yourself that you're going to have puppies.

Dehydration and Heat Stroke

Dehydration can occur during any season. Signs of dehydration and heat stroke include elevated temperature, extreme thirst, watery diarrhea, vomiting, lethargy, high temperature (over 103°F), skin around muzzle or neck that does not snap back when pinched, difficulty breathing, weakness, and pale gums.

Do not muzzle the dog. Move him into the shade or a cool and well-ventilated area. Give your Lab cool water or unflavored pediatric electrolyte to drink. Soak the dog in tepid or cool water. Do not use ice-cold water because it will cause the capillaries to contract and not dissipate heat. Make certain the dog can breathe—remove constricting collars or other items. Obtain immediate veterinary attention.

Prevent heat stroke by keeping your Lab in well-ventilated areas with shade in the summertime. Always provide fresh water. Do not exercise your Lab in hot weather. Never leave a dog in a car during warm weather, even with the windows down.

Electrical Shock

Do not touch your dog or you might be shocked also. Use a wooden broom handle or other nonconductive item to unplug the cord. Treat as you would for traumatic shock by maintaining proper body temperature and seek emergency veterinary treatment. Administer mouth-to-mouth resuscitation by closing the dog's mouth and breathing into its nose if the dog is not breathing.

Fishhooks

Fishhooks are nasty. If your Lab has stepped on one or had one pierce her lips, bring her to a vet. If no vet is available, you may have to muzzle your Lab and look for where the hook's barb is. Push the barb through the skin if necessary to expose it and then snip it off with a pair of wire cutters. Then remove the hook. Contact your vet; he or she may wish to prescribe antibiotics. Only your veterinarian should remove swallowed fishhooks.

Frostbite and Hypothermia

Signs of hypothermia include lowered body temperature, shivering, and lethargy, followed by stupor, shock, unconsciousness, and finally death. Lack of food for energy and dehydration can greatly affect your Lab's ability to keep warm. Dogs expend energy and heat while working, but if the heat loss is too great, your Lab may experience hypothermia.

Treatment for hypothermia is mostly common sense. Warm your Lab slowly by wrapping him in blankets or lying next to him in blankets to help warm him. If he is conscious, you should offer him warm broth to drink. Seek immediate veterinary attention.

Frostbite is where the skin is damaged as a result of cold. The skin will turn white if frostbitten. If severely frostbitten, the skin will actually turn black. Sometimes the affected skin will slough, leaving a raw sore. If the skin is white and intact, warm it slowly in tepid water (not hot—you can damage the skin further). It will be painful to warm the skin. In frostbite with sores, wrap with an antibiotic ointment and gauze. In all cases of frostbite, seek veterinary attention.

Insect Bites and Stings

You can treat most insect bites and stings with an over-the-counter antihistamine that your veterinarian can recommend. If your Lab shows any allergic reactions to bites or stings, (severe swelling or difficulty breathing), seek immediate veterinary attention. This can be a life-threatening condition known as an anaphylactic reaction.

Spider bites can be very serious. The two most dangerous spiders are the black widow and the brown recluse. Both of these spider bites can be fatal if left untreated. If you suspect a spider has bitten your Lab, seek veterinary attention.

Poisoning

Contact your veterinarian or local poison-control center and have available the substance or chemical that your dog has ingested so that you can properly describe the poison. Follow the veterinarian or poison-control center's instructions. Do not induce vomiting unless told to do so. Some acids, alkalis, and other substances can harm your dog more if they come back up.

Lab Bites

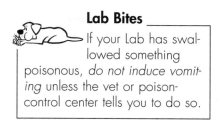

If your Lab has swallowed something poisonous, *do not induce vomiting* unless the vet or poison-control center tells you to do so.

The Least You Need to Know

- Labs are susceptible to hereditary conditions such as bloat/gastric torsion, cold tail, hip and elbow dysplasia, OCD, epilepsy, eye disease, hypothyroidism, HMLR, and TVD.
- Common illnesses and injuries to watch for include allergies, broken toenails, diarrhea and vomiting, foxtails, hot spots, incontinence, pyometra, and skunk sprays.
- Most emergencies require veterinary attention, but you can do things to help improve your Lab's chances of survival.

Chapter 19

The Golden Years

In This Chapter

- Learn how to keep your Lab active and healthy for a long life
- Learn how to keep your older Lab comfortable despite arthritis and other signs of aging
- Should you get a new puppy as your other dog ages?
- Euthanasia and grief

We all hate the thought of getting old, but the current alternatives are pretty grim. Someday, you'll notice that your dog is graying around the muzzle, or perhaps he's a little stiff when he gets up in the morning. Someday, you'll wake up and your Lab will be old.

This isn't a time for sadness; it's a time to enjoy each other. Dogs can and do live healthy and physically active lives over the age of 10. It's very possible—I've had several dogs who have lived to 14 or 15 years old. Part of the credit for longevity is due to genetics, but part is also due to medical care, diet, and being physically active. You can't change genetics, but you can make a crucial difference in your Lab's health and longevity.

In this chapter, I focus on the old dog. Yes, he's more susceptible to cancers and tumors, but he's also more fun to be around. Gone are the stupid puppy days; now you can enjoy your best friend. I cover how to make your Lab more comfortable and whether you should bring a new dog in at this time. I'll also cover the eventuality of euthanasia and how to know when it's your Lab's time.

Active Mind + Active Body = Healthy, Long Life

One day you'll wake up and realize that your Lab is old. Maybe it's that graying on the muzzle that you swore wasn't there yesterday. Maybe your Lab has decided that sleeping in is better than waking you up. Maybe he's a little stiff getting up. Whatever it is, you now know you have an old dog.

Lab Facts

When is old in a Lab? It depends. Just as some people don't seem old even when they're in their 70s, some Labs don't seem old when others are. Good genetics and a lifetime of exercise, good nutrition, and medical care can make the difference.

Many pet books place "seniors" at seven years or greater. But Labs can live to 13 to 15 years old with good care. From 8 to 10 years old, your Lab will start showing more changes due to old age. After 10, I would start calling the dog a senior.

Senior Activities

Just because your Lab is old, doesn't mean he's ready for the rocking chair on the porch. If your Lab has been healthy and active, there's no reason he shouldn't continue being healthy and active. In fact, if you start taking away his activities, you may find that he'll start deteriorating faster.

Keep an eye on your Lab when you work or exercise him. He may not be able to do everything a younger dog can, so don't insist on the same physical abilities of a younger dog. But don't retire him yet, either, unless he has a medical problem or injury that precludes the activity. Some older dogs enjoy a scaled-down version of the activity—it allows them to have fun and interact with you.

Feeding the Older Dog

Feed your Lab according to his weight and activity level. Don't necessarily switch him over to a "senior" diet unless he's gaining weight, his activity level has decreased, or he has a physical condition that warrants a change in dog food. Many of my "senior" dogs still work and are active—and get premium performance dog food.

Lab Bites

Older dogs are more prone to tumors and cancers. Examine your Lab for tumors and bring him to the vet if you find one. Cancer is a little harder to diagnose without running tests. If your Lab is eating but losing weight, drinking excessive water, tiring easily, or not eating well at all, take him to the vet for a full examination.

Keeping Your Old Lab Comfortable

Older dogs tend to enjoy a nice warm bed. Dogs who formerly eschewed the comforts of home tend to enjoy them now. A soft bed made from orthopedic foam can help relieve pressure points. Some pet equipment manufacturers have developed electric heating mats that radiate constant warmth for the dog. If you do use one of these, be certain that the cord is hidden so that your Lab can't chew it and accidentally be shocked.

The stairs that were once an obstacle only when your Lab was a small puppy now may become a real problem. If you can, move his crate or bed to the lower part of the house so that he doesn't have to climb stairs anymore, or install a ramp.

As your Lab gets older, he may have trouble chewing his food. Moistening his dog food or feeding him canned food is an alternative that will help make your Lab more comfortable.

Coping with Loss of Senses

If your Lab acts as if he's ignoring you, he may be going deaf. Deafness can come on gradually or suddenly. Clap your hands behind your Lab's head or rattle the food bowl while he's in the other room. If he doesn't react, he's probably deaf. Start using hand signals to show your Lab what you want him to do. It may take a little bit of time for him to pick up on it.

You may not even notice if your Lab goes blind. Most dogs are quite adept at getting around their home and even their neighborhood even though they're blind. The owner usually notices something is amiss when the dog bumps into something that normally isn't there. Have your vet confirm your suspicions if you think your Lab is blind.

Now is not the time to rearrange the furniture. Keep your Lab at home and in familiar surroundings if he is blind or impaired visually. Don't let him off the leash or he might wander around and become lost. When in a strange place, keep him beside you—you are his seeing-eye person now!

Arthritis

Arthritis seems a constant in age—for both people and dogs. If your Lab is not active, you may see signs of arthritis early. Some supplements, such as Glucosamine and MSM (found in Cosequin, Glycoflex, or Synova-Cre), can help relieve arthritis. These supplements work well on some dogs and do nothing for others. Your Lab usually has to be on it for over six weeks before you can see any effect.

Your vet can help mitigate some of the effects of arthritis with anti-inflammatories such as aspirin. Do not give your dog analgesics such as acetaminophen or ibuprofen—they are very poisonous to dogs. Your vet can prescribe the right amount of buffered aspirin, anti-inflammatories, or steroids to alleviate pain and swelling.

> **Lab Bites**
>
> Never give analgesics such as acetaminophen or ibuprofen to your Lab. These are very poisonous to dogs. Talk to your vet about anti-inflammatories and the proper dosages.

Should You Get a Second Dog?

Some people decide to get a puppy as their Lab ages. The idea is to help mitigate the pain of losing the beloved pet when the time finally arrives. This can be good or bad, depending on the circumstance. If your Lab is very old, he may look on this new puppy as an interloper. A puppy will take most of your time and energy—leaving little time for your old dog. Your Lab may feel neglected and may become aggressive or short-tempered with your new pup.

However, some dogs tolerate puppies well. Sometimes a puppy can spark new life into an old dog. Something new and exciting can shake an old dog from the routine enough to make him feel young again. Some older dogs are quick to become the puppy's aunt or uncle, and are delighted to "show the ropes" to the newcomer.

> **Retriever Rewards**
>
> If you decide to bring another dog or a puppy into the family, always choose a neutral area such as a park for your Lab to meet him. Let your Lab greet the newcomer while on the leash. Praise your Lab for good behavior and discourage bad behavior. It may take a few sessions before you can let your Lab loose with the other dog or puppy.

Whether another dog or puppy is accepted largely depends on you and your Lab. If your Lab gets along with other dogs and puppies, perhaps getting a puppy might be the right choice. At the same time, you must take the time to make your Lab feel extra special. Don't stop doing things with her now that you have the puppy—otherwise she will associate the lack of attention with the appearance of the interloper.

Saying Good-Bye

Saying good-bye is perhaps the hardest thing to do as a dog owner. I've had to put several of my dogs down now and the truth is, it doesn't get any easier. Nor is the decision always clear cut.

Sometimes it's obvious: your Lab is in great pain and is dying from a terminal disease or injury. Other times, the diagnosis is unclear, or you're sitting in an emergency room and don't know what to do. Heroic efforts may be required to save him, which cost far beyond what you can afford; and your Lab might have a very slim chance of recovery anyway. In times like this, talk to someone you can trust—perhaps your own vet, or you might obtain a second opinion. Other friends who are dog owners may be able to see clearly when you cannot. They may offer you advice untainted by the emotions of the situation.

An End to Suffering

Don't allow your best friend to suffer needlessly. While it is tempting to try heroic actions to save your pet, you may discover that the end result is still the same. Dogs don't live forever and even though you want your Lab to live a little longer, it may not be humane or in anyone's capability.

Euthanasia is painless and quick. The veterinarian will administer an injection and your pet will be gone. You can stay with your Lab during his final minutes or leave—your choice. Many pet owners opt to stay with their dog during the last few minutes because it brings closure.

Good Grief!

You will grieve. This is normal and natural. Don't talk to non-dog owners about it because they will be the most callous. They may tell you it was only a pet. No, it wasn't. Your Lab was your friend and it would be callous to not grieve for a good friend who just died.

Talk to your vet about grief. He or she may be able to refer you to free or low-cost pet loss counseling. Many veterinary colleges or humane societies offer free or low-cost pet loss hotlines. Take care of yourself during this time. Keep busy and active—exercise and eat a balanced diet. Avoid being alone and going into depression. You aren't denying that you have grief over the loss—you are helping yourself deal with it.

With time, the pain and anguish of your pet's death will fade. You will start remembering all the good times you had together. Perhaps, in time, you'll be ready to own another Labrador Retriever. Perhaps you will get a puppy to keep you occupied. If you do, remember that no puppy will replace your beloved pet and that no dog will be like your Lab. Your new puppy or dog will have a different personality and different behaviors—do not expect the same thing out of this puppy. However, in time, you may grow to love this new addition as much as your beloved pet.

Retriever Rewards

An excellent pet loss site on the Internet is www.petloss.com. It has some of the most comprehensive lists of pet loss support groups, hotlines, and information to be found anywhere.

The Least You Need to Know

- Keeping your older dog active will help him lead a longer, better life.
- Your old lab will need your help coping with arthritis, blindness, deafness, and other old-age ills.
- Carefully consider getting a new puppy as your dog ages.
- You will grieve when your Lab dies. Don't let him suffer needlessly just to postpone the inevitable.

Appendix A

Glossary

AAFCO The Association of Animal Feed Control Officials.

agility A sport where dogs go through a specially designed obstacle course. It is a timed event, so dogs that complete the course accurately in the least amount of time do well.

alpha When trainers talk about "alpha," they are talking about who is "in charge."

alpha dog A dog that has a dominant personality.

American Kennel Club (or AKC) The AKC is the oldest and largest national registry for purebred dogs in the United States. The AKC was founded in 1884.

article An item impregnated with scent used for tracking.

bait pouches Bait pouches are little pouches that enable you to carry your treats if you don't have pockets or if you don't want to get your pockets messy. They're called "bait" because when you stack a dog in conformation, you lure or "bait" him with a treat so that he will look attentive.

CD Companion Dog title.

CDX Companion Dog Excellent title.

Champion Abbreviated CH. A dog that earns 15 points in conformation dog shows.

clean run An agility run without faults.

clicker training A form of positive reinforcement that relies heavily on operant conditioning. When he does something right, the dog hears a click from a special clicker and is conditioned to expect a treat. Dogs quickly learn to do things that will cause the click (and the subsequent treat) and avoid behaviors that will not produce the click.

conformation The structure of the dog as it conforms to the breed standard.

congenital A condition that is present at birth that may have either genetic or environmental causes.

contact obstacle An agility obstacle that the dog must climb up on and travel across; that is, make contact with. Contact obstacles frequently have zones that the dog must touch to avoid disqualification.

correct To cause unwanted behavior to cease.

Dual Champion Abbreviated DC. A dog that has its CH and FC titles.

Field Trial Champion Abbreviated FC. A hunting title obtained when the dog wins either a National Championship Stake or 10 points in Open All-Age, Limited All-Age, Special All-Age, or Restricted All-Age competition.

foxtails Also called grass awns; sticky seeds that bury into a dog's coat and skin. They can bury themselves into the body, causing abscesses.

free feeding To leave the food out all the time so that your dog can eat it whenever he chooses.

Gamblers A type of agility course offered. The dog accumulates points in Gamblers for a set amount of time. When the judge blows the whistle, the dog must complete the "Gamble" or mandatory sequence.

Heel position A position where your dog sits or stands beside your left side, right next to your knee.

hereditary A condition that is genetic; that is, inherited through the genes of the parents.

hip dysplasia A crippling hereditary disease. This is a prevalent condition among many breeds, including Labrador Retrievers. The hip socket is malformed and the ball and socket that make up the hip doesn't fit properly, causing limping and great pain. Severe cases of hip dysplasia require expensive surgery that can cost thousands of dollars. Extreme cases of hip dysplasia may require euthanasia.

hobbyist breeders Another name for reputable breeders.

ILP Indefinite Listing Privilege registration allows a purebred dog without a full registration to compete in AKC competitive sports such as obedience. You must spay or neuter your Lab and have a veterinarian, breeder, or trainer sign stating that the dog appears to be the breed you're applying for.

Jumpers Class In agility, Jumpers Class has only hurdles and tunnels on the course, making it a very fast course for the dog to travel across.

Jumpers with Weaves A special class in AKC agility. It is similar to the Jumpers class of USDAA and NADAC, except it has weave poles in the course.

leg A leg in competition means a qualifying score in one day's competition or event. You can earn legs in obedience, agility, tracking, and other competitive sports. In tracking, a distinct segment of the course.

limited-slip collar A slip collar that has a restriction that prevents the collar from tightening too much.

meat by-products The non-rendered, clean parts, other than meat, from slaughtered mammals. It includes all organs and defatted fatty tissues. It does not include the contents of the stomach or intestine, hair, horns, teeth, or hooves.

meat meal The meat has water and fat extracted. If the label says "chicken meal," the meal must be made from chickens.

microfilariae Heartworm larvae that infect a dog.

NADAC North American Dog Agility Council.

nutraceuticals A nutritional supplement intended to help mitigate a condition or disease.

off-course In agility, a dog incurs an off-course penalty if he takes the wrong obstacle in the sequence or enters the obstacle from the wrong side.

omega dog A dog who is very submissive and tentative; the lowest in the dog pack hierarchy.

over-angulation Where the angulation is greater than what is appropriate for proper conformation.

pedigree A dog's family tree.

pet quality A pet-quality puppy or dog is a dog that has a superficial blemish or "fault" that would prevent him from competing in the conformation (dog) show ring.

polygenic A trait or condition coming from more than one gene pair.

positive reinforcement A training technique that rewards the dog for behaving in the correct manner. It is a form of operant conditioning that uses little, if any, coercion or punishment. Both owners and dogs enjoy this training.

Progressive Retinal Atrophy A genetic eye condition that leads to blindness.

prong collar A training collar made from steel links with prongs that turn inside against the dog's neck. This collar is a limited-slip design; when pulled, it will cause the prongs to grab into the loose folds of skin around the neck.

quick The portion of a dog's nail with blood vessels that supply the nail.

refusal In agility, a dog incurs a refusal penalty (AKC only) if the dog passes the obstacle or heads toward the obstacle and then turns away.

relay A type of agility course where a team runs the course in relays.

reputable breeder A reputable breeder breeds dogs for the betterment of the breed. These breeders perform tests on their dogs to avoid breeding puppies with bad hips, hereditary blindness, or other inherited diseases. These breeders guarantee their dogs and often screen their puppy buyers rigorously. They do not always have available puppies.

retriever A type of dog used to retrieve game. Labradors are one type of Retriever recognized by the AKC.

sequencing In agility, putting several obstacles in a sequence to learn how to handle the dog in the most efficient manner.

show quality A show-quality puppy or dog is a dog that conforms closely to standard and may be competitive in a conformation (dog) show.

slip collar A collar, used for training purposes, usually made from chain. This collar tightens when pulled.

snap choke A type of slip collar that snaps onto a loose ring. It is made of parachute cord rather than steel links and offers more control than the standard slip collar.

snooker A type of agility course offered through USDAA, set up in a modified snooker pattern.

stack Standing one's dog in the conformation show ring to emphasize positive characteristics and diminish flaws.

standard A kind of blueprint for the breed. We say a dog *conforms to the standard* when he meets the size, appearance, movement, and temperament requirements set by the AKC for that breed.

Standard Class An agility class that has contact obstacles, hurdles, and tunnels.

static mats Low-shock mats that give a jolt similar to walking across a carpeted area and touching a doorknob. (Yes, I've touched one. They're unpleasant, but harmless.) These mats are far less painful than if your Lab burns himself trying to steal food off the stove.

stud book A book that lists all dogs that were bred. This is maintained by the AKC and the breed clubs.

track The tracking "course" where the dogs follow the scent that the tracklayer has laid down.

tracking leads Leashes made from cotton or nylon that can be anywhere from 10 to 30 feet in length. Trainers use these leads for tracking work (hence the name) but also for distance work such as working on the "Recall" command.

trial A single competition, where your dog may compete once for a qualifying score.

trichinosis A parasitic disease that can cause serious illness and even death.

tularemia A bacterial infection that is characterized by high fever, loss of appetite, stiffness, and lethargy.

UD Utility Dog title.

USDAA The United States Dog Agility Association.

weave poles Weave poles are 1-inch PVC pipe poles in sets of 6 to 12 poles set anywhere from 18 to 25 inches apart in a straight line. The dog must enter the weave poles and weave through them (hence the name).

Appendix B

Organizations for Lab Owners

Agility Association of Canada (AAC)
RR #2
Lucan, Ontario
N0N2J0
519-657-7636

American Kennel Club (AKC)
5580 Centerview Drive
Raleigh, NC 27606-3390
919-233-9767
Website: www.akc.org
E-mail: info@akc.org

AKC Companion Animal Recovery
5580 Centerview Dr., Ste. 250
Raleigh, NC 27606-3389
1-800-252-7894
Website: www.akccar.org

Canine Backpackers Association LLC (Hiking and Backpacking)
PO Box 934
Conifer, CO 80433
303-679-7359
Website: www.caninebackpackers.org

Canine Eye Registration Foundation (CERF)
Department of Veterinary Clinical Science
School of Veterinary Medicine
Purdue University
West Lafayette, IN 47907
765-494-8179
Fax: 765-494-9981
Website: www.vet.purdue.edu/~yshen/cerf.html/

Canine Freestyle Federation
Monica Patty, Corresponding Secretary
21900 Foxden Lane
Leesburg, VA 20175
Website: www.canine-freestyle.org
E-mail: secretary@canine-freeestyle.org

The Labrador Retriever Club
Christopher Wincek, Secretary
9690 Wilson Mill Rd.
Chardon, OH 44024
Website: www.thelabradorclub.com
E-mail: rodarbal@aol.com

National Dog Registry
Box 116
Woodstock, NY 12498
1-800-637-3647
Website: www.natldogregistry.com

North American Flyball Association, Inc.
1400 W. Devon Ave, #512
Chicago, IL 60660
309-688-9840
Website: www.flyballdogs.com/flyball.html
E-mail: flyball@flyball.org

Orthopedic Foundation for Animals (OFA)
2300 Nifong Boulevard
Columbia, MO 65201
573-442-0418
Website: www.offa.org

PennHIP
Synbiotics Corporation
11011 Via Frontera
San Diego, CA 92127
858-451-3771
Fax: 858-451-5719
Website: www.synbiotics.com/html/chd_penn_hip.html

Tattoo-A-Pet
6571 S.W. 20th Court
Ft. Lauderdale, FL 33317
1-800-828-8667
Website: www.tattoo-a-pet.com

United Kennel Club (UKC)
100 East Kilgore Road
Kalamazoo, MI 49001-5593
Website: www.ukcdogs.com

United States Dog Agility Association (USDAA)
PO Box 850955
Richardson, TX 75085-0955
972-231-9700
Information Line: 1-888-AGILITY
Website: www.usdaa.com
E-mail: info@usdaa.com

World Canine Freestyle Organization Ltd.
PO Box 250122
Brooklyn, NY 11235
718-332-8336
Fax: 718-646-2686
Website: www.woofs.org/wcfo/
E-mail: wcfodogs@aol.com

Appendix C

Periodicals and Books

Periodicals

AKC Gazette
51 Madison Ave.
New York, NY 10010

Clean Run
Monica Percival and Linda Mechlenburg
35 Walnut Street
Turner Falls, MA 01376
413-863-8308
Website: www.cleanrun.com
E-mail: info@cleanrun.com

Dog Fancy Magazine
P.O. Box 53264
Boulder, CO 80322-3264
1-800-365-4421
Website: www.dogfancy.com

Dog World
P.O. Box 56240
Boulder, CO 80323-6240
1-800-361-8056

Finish Line
Melanie McAvoy
1002 E. Samuel Avenue
Peoria Heights, IL 61614
309-682-7617
E-mail: melmcavoy@worldnet.att.net

Front & Finish
P.O. Box 333
Galesburg, IL 61402-0333
309-344-1333
Fax: 309-344-1165
Website: www.frontandfinish.com

Gun Dog
P.O. Box 343
Mt. Morris, IL 61054-0343
1-800-800-7724

Just Labs
570 Howell Avenue
Cincinnati, OH 45220
Website: www.justlabradors.com

The Labrador Quarterly
4401 Zephyr Street
Wheat Ridge, CO 80033-2499

Off-Lead
100 Bouck St.
Rome, NY 13440

The Retriever Journal
P.O. Box 509
Traverse City, MI 49685
1-800-447-7367
Website: www.retrieverjournal.com

Books

Alderton, David. *The Dog Care Manual.* Hauppauge, N.Y.: Barron's Educational Series, 1986.

American Kennel Club. *The Complete Dog Book*, 19th ed. New York: Howell Book House, 1997.

Baer, Ted. *Communicating with Your Dog*. Hauppauge, N.Y.: Barron's Educational Series, 1989.

Bailey, Gwen. *The Well-Behaved Dog*. Hauppauge, N.Y.: Barron's Educational Series, 1998.

Benjamin, Carol Lea. *Second-Hand Dog*. New York: Howell Book House, 1988.

Bloeme, Peter. *Frisbee Dogs: How to Raise, Train, and Compete.* Atlanta, Ga.: Skyhoundz, 1994.

Bonham, Margaret H. *An Introduction to Dog Agility*. Hauppauge, N.Y.: Barron's Educational Series, 2000.

———. *The Simple Guide to Getting Active with Your Dog*. Neptune City, N.J.: TFH Publications Inc, 2002.

Burnham, Patricia Gail. *Play Training Your Dog*. New York: St. Martin's Press, 1986.

Coffman, Howard D. *The Dry Dog Food Reference*. Nashua, N.H.: Pig Dog Press, 1995.

Elliot, Rachel Page. *The New Dogsteps*. New York: Howell Book House, 1983.

Giffin, James M., MD, and Liisa D. Carlson, DVM. *The Dog Owner's Home Veterinary Handbook*, 3d ed. New York: Howell Book House, 2000.

Gilbert, Edward M. Jr., and Thelma R. Brown. *K-9 Structure and Terminology*. New York: Howell Book House, 1995.

Handler, Barbara, and Betty J. McKinney. *Successful Obedience Handling: The New Best Foot Forward*. Loveland, Colo.: Alpine Publications, 1991.

Hinchcliff, Kenneth W. B.V.Sc., M.S., Ph.D., Diplomate ACVIM, Gregory A. Reinhart, Ph.D., and Arleigh J. Reynolds. *Performance Dog Nutrition*. Dayton, Ohio: The Iams Company, 1999.

Holst, Phyllis A. M.S., D.V.M. *Canine Reproduction, A Breeder's Guide*. Loveland, Colo.: Alpine Publications, 1985.

Hutchins, Jim, HOGA Agility. *Do-It-Yourself Plans for Constructing Dog Agility Articles*. Jackson, Miss.: HOGA Agility, 1999.

James, Ruth B. D.V.M. *The Dog Repair Book*. Mills, Wyo.: Alpine Press, 1990.

Klever, Ulrich. *The Complete Book of Dog Care*. Hauppauge, N.Y.: Barron's Educational Series, 1989.

LaBelle, Charlene. *A Guide to Backpacking with Your Dog*. Loveland, Colo.: Alpine Publications, 1993.

Merck and Co. *The Merck Veterinary Manual*, Seventh Edition. Whitehouse Station, N.J.: Merck and Co, Inc., 1991.

Olson, Lonnie. *Flyball Racing: The Dog Sport for Everyone*. New York: Howell Book House, 1997.

Papurt, M. L. *Saved! A Guide to Success with Your Shelter Dog*. Hauppauge, N.Y.: Barron's Educational Series, 1997.

Pryor, Karen. *Don't Shoot the Dog! The New Art of Teaching and Training*. New York: Bantam Doubleday Dell, 1999.

Ralston Purina Compan.y.. *Purina's Complete Guide to Nutrition, Care, and Health for Your Dog and Cat*. St. Louis, Mo.: Ralston Purina Company.

Smith, Cheryl S., and Stephanie J. Tauton. *The Trick Is in the Training*. Hauppauge, N.Y.: Barron's Educational Series, 1998.

Streitferdt, Uwe. *Healthy Dog, Happy Dog*. Hauppauge, N.Y.: Barron's Educational Series, 1994.

Volhard, Joachim, Wendy Volhard, and Jack Volhard. *The Canine Good Citizen: Every Dog Can Be One*. New York: Howell Book House, 1997.

Wrede, Barbara J. *Civilizing Your Puppy*, 2d ed., Hauppauge, N.Y.: Barron's Educational Series, 1997.

Zink, M. Chris D.V.M. Ph.D. *Peak Performance, Coaching the Canine Athlete*. New York: Howell Book House, 1992.

Index

A

B

C

D

E

F

G

H

I

J-K

L

M

N

O

P

Q-R

S

T

U-V

W-X-Y-Z